FIELD GUIDE TO

FISH
LURES

IDENTIFICATION
&
VALUE GUIDE

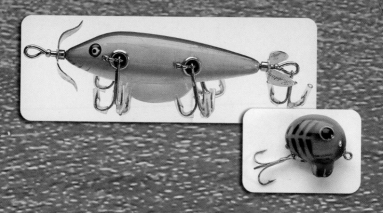

Russell E. Lewis

COLLECTOR BOOKS
A Division of Schroeder Publishing Co., Inc.

Front cover, from top: Ropher Fin-Dingo, Allcock Spinner, Shakespeare Evolution, Heddon Crab Wiggler, Creek Club Pikie, in rare Fireplug color.

Back cover, left: Ropher Fin-Dingo, Heddon 151 (Dowagiac Minnow) in Rainbow.

Cover design by Beth Summers
Book design by Joyce A. Cherry
Photos by Russell E. Lewis

COLLECTOR BOOKS
P.O. Box 3009
Paducah, Kentucky 42002-3009
www.collectorbooks.com

Copyright © 2005 Russell E. Lewis

The current values in this book should be used only as a guide. They are not intended to set prices, which vary from one section of the country to another. Auction prices as well as dealer prices vary greatly and are affected by condition as well as demand. Neither the author nor the publisher assumes responsibility for any losses that might be incurred as a result of consulting this guide.

Searching For A Publisher?

We are always looking for people knowledgeable within their fields. If you feel that there is a real need for a book on your collectible subject and have a large comprehensive collection, contact Collector Books.

Contents

Dedication

Dedicated to all of those who have gone before us attempting to invent a better lure for fishing and leaving behind a legacy for collecting.

All of my efforts are only possible due to the constant support of my dear wife, Wendy. It is to her that this work is sincerely dedicated. She is the one that puts up with fishing lures from floor to ceiling, photos throughout the house, and her husband missing for hours on end while taking photos or writing about fishing lures. Thanks again, Wendy!

But, I would also like to dedicate this work in memoriam to my last two co-authors: Carl F. Luckey and Clyde A. Harbin, "The Bassman." I was fortunate enough to be involved with books that both of these men brought to collectors very early on in the collecting of fishing lures. They were both pioneers in the field. I was doubly fortunate to be allowed to continue their efforts through my own writings, and for this I am most grateful.

So, to the memories of Mr. Luckey and The Bassman I dedicate this work. Without pioneers such as these two men, lure collecting would still be in its infancy. Thanks for allowing me to be a small part of that history.

Introduction

This general field guide to collectible fishing lures is intended to assist the beginning and intermediate collector in identifying and appraising a wide variety of lures often encountered in the field. It is not meant to be an exhaustive compendium of all lure companies and values. Such a task would be impossible in a "field guide."

However, I have included enough basic information and selected photographs so even the inexperienced collector should be able to know a "good buy" from a "bad buy" out in the field. The most important elements in lure collecting are related to the maker of the lure and the condition of the lure. Specific models and colors also determine value. Finally, age is often a determining factor, but not as important as most believe.

Values given are general values for a range of lures shown and specific values for specific lures that I have sold. As many of you know from buying *Captain John's Fishing Tackle Price Guide*, by John A. Kolbeck and myself, published by Collector Books in 2003, I have kept track of each and every sale made online, at shows and by private sale. If you want to see 10,000 plus actual prices by lure maker, color, model, and condition, pick up that book. However, it does not really identify the lures in detail for the beginner. This guide should be more helpful to the beginner, and the two books used in conjunction should answer most questions as to value.

It is my opinion that there are six lure companies in greatest demand across America. Listed alphabetically they are Creek Chub Bait Company, Heddon, Paw Paw, Pflueger, Shakespeare, and South Bend. Listed in order of demand the first two would be Heddon and then Creek Chub Bait Company. Any of these companies, however, are in high demand by collectors and as a general rule result in the strongest prices for their lures.

I cannot give a history of each company presented in this book and have it be a "field guide," so readers will have to seek out wisdom elsewhere. I have written a number of books on fishing lure history and collecting.

My main series of books is the *Modern Fishing Lure Collectibles* series also published by Collectors Books. Volumes 1 and 2 are in print and Volume 3 is scheduled for release in early 2005. Volumes 4 and 5 will complete the series by the end of 2006. These five volumes detail the history and lures for hundreds of companies from 1937 until the

1980s. Luckey's book is an excellent beginning history, White's multiple photo type volumes are helpful, Slade's book is detailed and has a number of smaller companies, and Murphy & Edmisten provide one of the finest photo essays of any fishing book. I recommend that the beginning collector invest in this guide and our *Captain John's Fishing Tackle Price Guide* first to learn about pricing. Once a person gets his/her feet wet, invest in some more books for more detail and knowledge. As all of the authors say, knowledge is power in lure collecting.

The format of this book is simple: I begin with the "big six" companies listed on page 5 and present them alphabetically. Each company has a brief introduction as to the lures in production in 1952 and collectors are given a benchmark reference point of lure types for the company. I then go on to add earlier lures (vintage) and even some later collectible lures (classic). I also provide a brief introduction on lure values for each company. Then, included for each company is a photo essay showing lures and values, either actual values based upon recent sales or a range based upon my experience of selling literally thousands of lures.

What I have attempted to give the reader is a general impression of a company, e.g. what do Creek Chub lures in general look like — shapes, types, colors, anything unusual, etc. What are typical Creek Chub lures? Are there any special colors to watch for in this company?

Will this book cover all lure companies and every collectible lure? No, this is impossible in such a guide. However, I have included the most likely lures to be found while searching for collectible lures in the field, at auctions, at flea markets, in garage sales, and in grandpa's tackle box. It should answer most of your beginning questions and hopefully keep you from believing all lures are worth the $30,000+ brought by a rare copper color Heddon 150 from 1904 in 2003 (online auction) or the $100,000+ brought for the rare Haskell Minnow at a Langley auction in 2003. Most (in terms of volume) collectible fishing lures start at $8.00 and go up to $20.00, period.

Actually, there are some general price ranges and they are inversely related to the commonality of achieving those prices. Most lures start at $8.00 and go to $20.00. Then, a fairly large number of lures will sell for $20.00 – $50.00 each. Far fewer lures muster the $50.00 to $100.00 mark. Now it starts getting tough to break $100.00; very few lures are worth $100.00 or more compared to the number of lures being collected. It takes a lure in fine condition, a rare model and/or color, and high collector appeal (Heddon 150s for example). However, many Heddon 150s are sold for less than $100.00. So, yes, there is a category of $100.00 to $500.00 covering most of the top of the line lures for the better companies. Also, there is a category of $500.00+ for all remaining lures; this includes only very special lures such as the Pflueger Muskellunge Minnow from the 1890s, great early Heddon lures in excellent condition, a rare color plastic that someone just had to have, or the rare Heddon 150 and Haskell minnow mentioned on page 6. Relatively few lures are worth more than $500.00.

One final introductory note on condition is in order here. The National Fishing Lure Collectors Club has a ten-point scale with 1 being the lowest and 10 being the highest in terms of condition. Most collectors use general terms such as mint, excellent, and very good, not meaning the same from one person to the next, but giving a general idea of condition. I have given values for lures on the high range of condition, e.g. excellent minus to mint in the box.

One huge mistake made by most new collectors is to forget the importance of condition. It cannot be understated how important it is to value. Value diminishes very rapidly as does condition. A poor lure is a poor lure and should bring only a small percentage of a mint lure's value. For instance, a common pikie color Creek Chub Pikie 700 in the common box is worth $20.00 – 30.00, as there were a million of them made. But, in poor shape it is worth a fraction of that price. Red/white Bass-Orenos by South Bend would be another example, or Heddon Yellow Shore Minnow River Runts. All common colors, all common lures, value diminishes fast with poor condition. Please keep this in mind. I know the fever of buying lures gets to us all, but please remember my basic law school term of *Caveat Emptor* (let the buyer beware).

One final Latin note: carpe diem. It means "seize the day." Sometimes we have to take a chance on a lure when in the field and one should know that often the lure will be gone when one returns. Sometimes we have to balance seizing the day with being wary so do not miss a vintage Heddon from 1920 at a fair price because the exact value is not known. After a while, you will get a feeling for a "good lure" just by handling lures and viewing a few hundred of the more collectible lures.

The main thing in lure collecting is not to turn it into a mathematical calculation with every purchase. I overpay for many items just because I want them. I have made some great buys along the way (my best is $85.00 for a $2,000.00+ Muskellunge Minnow). But regardless of the value, one should be collecting also for pleasure, a commodity that seldom has a price tag. Enjoy, and good luck!

The Big Six

As stated earlier, the lures of the big six companies will be presented first in alphabetical order. There is little doubt that the lures most people will encounter in their early searching will be from one of these six companies about 70% of the time at least.

Heddon is the most collected of any company and is closely followed by the Creek Chub Bait Company. Many collectors prefer Shakespeare, South Bend, Pflueger, or Paw Paw. But regardless of which company, they are all valued by most of us.

Each of the six companies has certain traits that make them usually identifiable even to a beginner. By studying lures and handling them one will quickly get a feel for the styles most often represented in any given company. There are difficult and unusual lures one will encounter in the major company lines; however, one will quickly recognize lures by color, type, and maker.

To amass a collection of the lures from the big six companies would take a lifetime and a large sum of money. However, one can certainly afford to gather together at least some fine examples from each of the major companies to admire.

Creek Chub Bait Company

This Garrett, Indiana, company started with the production of its famed Wiggler shown on page 15. Baits often associated with Creek Chub are the Pikie, the Plunker, the Darter, the Injured Minnow, the Dingbat series, and, of course, the Wiggler. Colors typifying Creek Chub include its famed Pikie color, Silver Flash, Golden Shiner, and early natural Chub colors on the Wigglers. A favored color is the Red Side on many lures. Rare color patterns include most black/white lures, blue/white lures, and the frog pattern on a number of them. There are also some rare colors in plastic lures and one should realize for example that a plastic Pikie (700-P) in Rainbow Trout will begin at $50.00. Most plastic Creek Chub lures still do not bring the prices of early Heddon plastic lures but some are in even greater demand depending on color and model. But, only a more advanced text will detail this for you.

I am printing at the beginning of each company section most of the lures in production in 1952 for two reasons. The first reason is that it will give a benchmark for collectors. The second reason is that by 1952 most companies had added both spinning lures and some plastic lures to their production lines. So, if a lure is on this list it is likely that it was a "vintage" wooden lure for the company at one time and may now be a lure transitioning into plastic or a new spinning size. But keep in mind that some lures were only made in plastic once invented, such as my favorite, the Fin-Dingo by Ropher and South Bend.

This listing of lures by company is further broken into two categories: spinning and metal lures in the first category and the traditional baitcasting plugs in the second category. Of course, some companies shown later will fall only within one of these two categories. I am simply trying to list for the reader in one handy spot all of the lures likely to be found made by one company in one of two categories. I hope this helps.

Creek Chub made only a few metal baits, its Cohokie of the late 1970s being a fine example. However, it entered the spinning tackle lure market with the making of the Injured Minnow in a ¼ oz. size, and the Spinning Darter, Spinning Pikie (straight and jointed), and Spinning Plunker, all in ¼ oz. sizes. All of the original Creek Chub spinning lures were made in wood and later became plastic. See my *Volume 1* for many examples in both wood and plastic.

Creek Chub lures are some of the most collectible of bait companies, and there are dozens of lure types made by the company. In 1952, it was still making lures in wood and had not yet added plastic versions of its traditional lures to the line. Surface lures included the Darter, a ½ oz., 3¾" lure, and it also came in a Midget size at ⅜ oz., 3" long, Jointed at ½ oz., 3¾" long, Spinnered at ½ oz., 3¾" long. The Injured Minnow was ½ oz., 3¾" long, the Baby Injured Minnow was ½ oz., 2¾" long, and the Husky Injured Minnow was 1½ oz., 5" long. The Plunker was ⅝ oz., 3" long, the Midget Plunker was ⅜ oz., 2¼" long, and the Husky Plunker was over an ounce in weight and 4¼" long. The Plunking Dinger was ⅝ oz., 4" long. The Skipper was ⅝ oz., 3" long (one of the less common baits by Creek Chub). The Surface Dingbat was ⅝ oz. and 1¾" long. Sinking, or sinking/floating lures, by Creek Chub included the Baby Chub Wiggler at ½ oz., 2¾". The Crawdad came in two sizes, ½ oz. and ¾ oz., 2½" and 2¾" long. The very collectible Deluxe Wagtail was ½ oz., 2¾". Another old Creek Chub bait, the Husky Musky Wiggler was 1½ oz., 5" long. The war addition, the Bomber or Kreeker, was ⅝ oz., 2⅞" long. The famous Pikie Minnow family included the Pikie at ¾ oz., 4¼"; the Jointed Pikie being ¾ oz., 4¼"; the Midget Pikie at ¼ oz., 2¾"; the Midget Jointed Pikie at ¼ oz., 2¾"; the Baby Pikie at ½ oz., 3¼"; the Baby Jointed Pikie at ½ oz., 3¼"; the Husky Pikie at 1½ oz., 6"; and the

Husky Jointed Pikie at 1½ oz., 6". The Plunker-like Pop 'N Dunk was ⅝ oz., 2¾" long. The Scamp was a heavily advertised Creek Chub lure that was ½ oz., 2½" long. The very collectible Beetle came in two sizes; the Beetle was ¾ oz., 2½" long and the Midget Beetle was ½ oz., 2" long. The Dingbat was ⅝ oz., 2" long and the Midget Dingbat was ½ oz., 1⅝" long. The Dinger was ½ oz., 4" long. The Seven Thousand Crawdad lure is very hard to find and was ¾ oz., 2¾" long. The Tiny Tim was a ½ oz., 1¾" long lure that is very collectible today. The famed Wiggler that started it all for Creek Chub was still available in wood, weighing 1 oz. at 3½" length. Finally, the Wiggle Fish at ¾ oz., 3½" length rounds out the Creek Chub offerings. In addition to the above, there were fly rod sizes of some of the lures available, all fairly rare to find. Also, the Pikie, Jointed Pikie, Baby Pikie, and Jointed Baby Pikie were also available with deep diving lips in 1952. The same is true for a deep diving Scamp version. My *Modern Fishing Lure Collectibles Volume 1*, shows many Creek Chub examples.

Crisp from the correct box, a 3208 Plunker, my favorite color and a favorite lure. With glass eyes, original hang tag from box, and order blank. This set would command a premium price starting at $100.00.

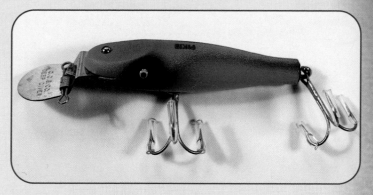

Rare color Fire Plug, Deep Diving Pikie, mint from box. $125.00+.

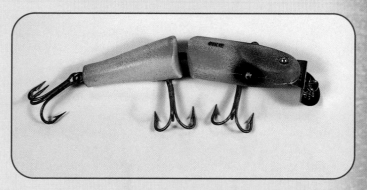

Compare this Rainbow Fire Jointed Pikie, Model 2600 with the rare color above. These colors are Gantron paint from only 1950 – 1953 and both are collectible and rare. (See also front cover.) $125.00+.

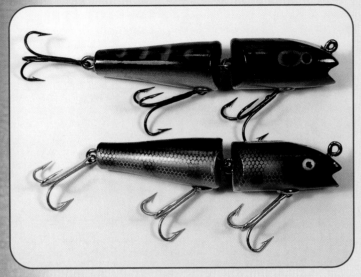

Top darter is typical later Creek Chub production with painted eyes, and bottom shows the same lure after Creek Chub moved to Iowa. Darters are very common and typify styling for the company. $15.00 – 20.00 each.

Top lure is a Model 1600 Baby Injured Minnow in plastic compared to the same lure in wood. Dace is a favorite collector color for Creek Chub. Wood, $40.00; plastic, $15.00.

Another stunning Creek Chub color is Golden Shiner in a beautiful lure called a Dinger from the late 1930s until the early 1950s. This Model 5600 lure brings a premium price and trades for $75.00 or better.

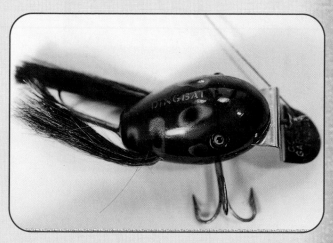

Most collectors like frog patterns and most Creek Chub collectors love the Dingbat lure. This glass-eyed frog Dingbat in excellent condition will trade for $75.00+ easily.

These photos show the older types of two-piece cardboard boxes for Creek Chub; the paper label boxes are more valuable. Paper label boxes, $20.00; standard stamped boxes, $10.00 (empty).

Top view of classic Creek Chub boxes. $10.00 – 20.00 each box, empty.

The bait that started Creek Chub, the classic Wiggler, with glass eyes, double line tie, nice scale pattern, evidence of "success." Early lures sell for $50.00+ depending on color, condition, etc., and some will reach very high values with lures in the $100.00 – 200.00 range being common.

One of the very few metal baits made by Creek Chub, a Model 1000 Cohokie, 2¾" long. This lure only lasted from 1968 – 1978. $25.00+.

Shur Strike lures offer a collector a wide range of collectible lures and boxes. $20.00+ for this empty box.

Note how this Shur-Strike Plunker is styled differently from the one shown earlier. The original Plunker also had this shape. $30.00 – 40.00.

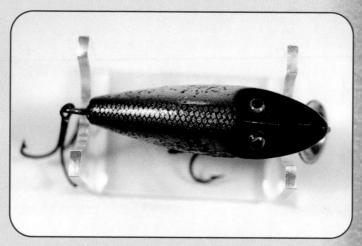

Two views of the Shur-Strike River Master, with glass eyes in silver flitter. $25.00.

Another rare find is any Creek Chub lure made by A, L & W, a Canadian affiliate of the company. A, L & W both made and jobbed Creek Chub lures, and finding them in early two-piece cardboard boxes such as this is prized. This Model 2600 Jointed Pikie in the ever popular Silver Flash color is especially nice. $125.00+.

Model 704 (straight Pikie) in Golden Shiner color, single line tie, glass eyes, excellent condition, with correct box. This sold in early 2004 for $40.00+.

Model 2604 (Jointed Pikie) in Golden Shiner color, single line tie, gold name stamped on back of lure, glass eyes, excellent shape, with early pocket catalog and box. This also sold for $40.00+ in early 2004.

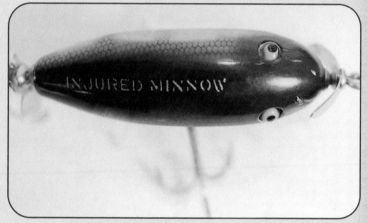

Top and bottom views of a Baby Injured Minnow in wood, glass eyes, name stamped on back, common Perch color, very good plus condition. Sold for $18.00 in early 2004.

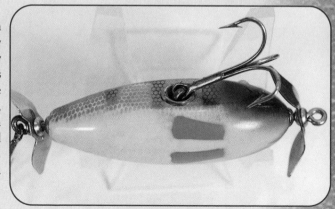

19

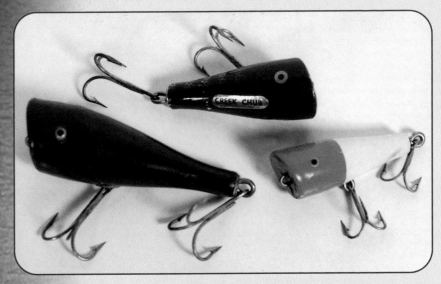

Three sizes of wooden Plunkers, all in used condition. Be careful of the solid black ones as they "repaint" easily and people will try to sell them as original when they are not! Also, note the label on the back of one. Creek Chub did not label lures ay first, but later gold stamped them, then added labels eventually. These three sold for $43.00 in early 2004.

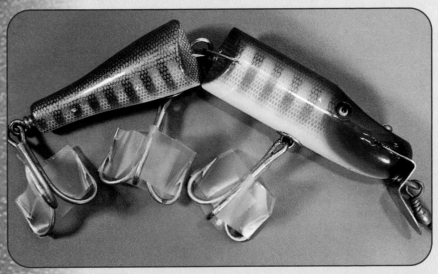

Large Snook Pikie in wood with glass eyes in excellent minus condition. Sold online in early 2004 for $38.00.

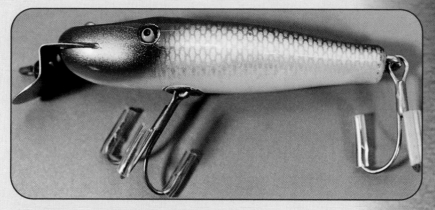

Baby Pikie in wood with glass eyes in white scale, a better color. $75.00 – 100.00.

Do not forget plastic lures. This rare color red head/pearl Baby Plunker in plastic is beautiful. Note the company name stamped into the lure. I paid $50.00 for this lure in April 2003 at a lure show.

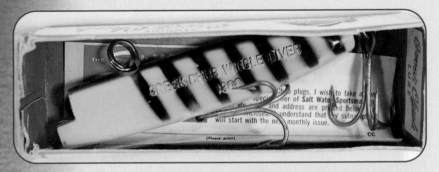

Wiggle Diver for saltwater fishing, new in box. $18.00 – 25.00.

A small but rare Creek Chub collection recently purchased by the author for $3,000.00. The top row shows one of the very popular and collectible Beetles in gold/yellow and the ever popular and rare Fintail Shiner. The second row shows Husky and Deluxe Wagtail Shiner lures in Perch and Golden Shiner colors with fluted tails followed by a Dinger in Frog. The bottom row shows a black Dinger, a Husky Dingbat in Pikie, and another gold/yellow Beetle in the smaller size.

Heddon

There is no doubt that more people collect Heddon lures than any other or that more has been written about the company than any other. I just completed a new edition, with the late Clyde Harbin, of his earlier book on Heddon lures called *Fifty Years of Heddon Catalogs*. Collector Books also has produced a fine book on Heddon history and lures. Luckey's book spends more time and pages on Heddon than any other company. My *Volume 1* dedicated 70 pages of 300 to Heddon. And the list continues from there.

One of the great advantages for collectors is that Heddon marked most of its lures, all but the earliest in most cases. I actually believe that is one reason so many people like Heddon — the lures are easy to identify. Obviously, the lures are also collected due to their outstanding quality of paint, design, and color. Once one handles an early Heddon versus an early "Brand X", the paint difference and varnish quality becomes obvious, with Heddon winning most contests in the comparison.

Values for Heddon lures go from the mundane common Black Shore River Runt Spook at $5.00 – 8.00 to the rare 1904 copper 150 selling for $30,000.00+ online in 2003. Most Heddon lures fall within the $20.00 – 50.00 range if in decent shape, and many will indeed exceed $100.00. A few of the rare vintage Heddon lures will exceed $500.00 and the record for high sales is held by Heddon for all but the super rare Haskell Minnow. I sell many Heddon plastic lures in the $12.00 – 40.00 range but it is not too often at this time in history to exceed $40.00 for most Heddon plastic lures.

One exception would be plastic Punkinseeds that still fetch $50.00 – 100.00 regularly, the tiny fly rod Punkinseed, Punkie Spooks bringing $125.00 – 200.00 each, many of the fly rod spook baits exceeding $50.00, and many of the Hi-Tails exceeding $50.00. Rare color Heddon River Runt Spooks have sold for hundreds of dollars as well, although most sell for less than $50.00 mint in the box. The best piece I have sold lately is one of the Dealer Dozen of River Runt Spooks as shown on page 28 for $1,000.00. This means the lures averaged about $83.33 each but they were all from 1947 – 1948 with mint pocket catalogs and mint in the box. The Dealer Dozen is a rare find and folks pay accordingly. I have also spent a bit on a Heddon lately trading another Dealer Dozen and about $400.00 cash for the metal tail Batwing Ice Decoy shown on page 27. These decoys sell for $1,500.00 – 4,000.00 depending on condition, location, and demand.

As for colors, Heddon made a number of special order colors for lures so any of them are worth more, e.g. non-standard colors not found in the catalogs for a particular lure. Also, blue scale is in general a rare color. Goldfish scale is not exceptionally rare but in high demand; the same is true for Rainbow. There are also rare plastic lure colors too numerous to document here but one example includes the common Black Shore being rare on Punkinseeds and Dowagiac Spooks.

There are a ton of Heddon lures on the market worth no more than $20.00 each and many collectors and dealers alike overprice Heddons due to the general demand. But remember that a Heddon in poor condition is still a poor lure. Condition is no less important in collecting Heddon lures than any other brand. So, here is a look at what Heddon had available in 1952 as a beginning point. Then photos and values are shown for Heddon lures more than any other company in this guide due to its importance in lure collecting.

Heddon entries into spoon type baits included the three sizes of Heddon Stanley baits known as the Ace, the Queen, and the King. The company also made for a short while a Devil's Bug in the same sizes in metal that is seldom seen. All of these early Heddon baits were made for baitcasting. Heddon introduced in 1952 its Tiny Trio of spinning lures, the Tiny Torpedo at ⅕ oz., 2⅛", Tiny Lucky 13 at ⅕ oz., 1⅞", and Tiny Runt at ⅕ oz., 2⅛". The Widget was a wooden fly rod lure but could be used for spinning with the addition of a spinner that was also introduced in 1952.

Regarding the traditional casting plugs there is little dispute that Heddon lures are the most collectible of all major lure companies. Heddon went into commercial production in 1901 with its first catalogs being printed in 1902. Heddon was an early experimenter in plastics with the Pyralin Luny Frog and the "Spook" baits made of Tenite 1 and Tenite 2 in the 1930s and 1940s. By 1952, Heddon had converted many of its vintage baits to plastic Spooks and had also introduced some spinning sizes as noted earlier. However, Heddon continued to make some baits in wood and even added new baits in wood during the 1950s, e.g. the Widget fly rod lure. The company also reintroduced many of the vintage wooden Heddon baits in the 1960s and then again as collector editions after Pradco bought them in 1984. In 1952 nearly all of the Heddon lures were still either baitcasting or fly rod versions, with only three specifically made for spinning, noted earlier. But, many versions were available and an endless color variation existed for Heddon baits, making them exciting to collect and always fun to fill in a color collection with a new find. Also, by 1952 surface rig was standard on Heddon lures, and painted eyes were often gold in color, but some white ones have been found.

Heddon surface baits in 1952 included the Chugger Spook at ½ oz., 3", and the Baby Chugger Spook at ⅜ oz., 2¼". One of the most collectible of all Heddon baits is the Crazy Crawler, still available in 1952 in both ⅝ oz. and ¾ oz. at 2⅜" and 2¾" lengths. These were models 2120 and 2100. They were shortly replaced by plastic and then only the 2120 size was made. The Flaptail was still made in wood at ¾ oz., 4" long, but was also available as a Flaptail Spook in ¾ oz., 3" length. The wooden Zaragossa, also known as the Old Zaragossa in 1952, was still available in ¾ oz., 4¼". The famed Zara Spook was available as a ¼ oz., 4¼" plastic version of this lure and the line tie was on the end of the mouth in 1952. The S.O.S. Wounded Minnow was ⅝ oz., 2⅞" long. The 210 Super Surface lure was a ¾ oz., 3½" old Heddon, still available. The Weedless Widow (former Wow) was ½ oz., 2⅜" long.

The Wounded Spook is one of the harder 1952 lures to find and was ⅝ oz. and 3⅞" long. My guess is that the Injured Minnow by Creek Chub so outsold the Wounded Spook that not many of them were sold. Heddon surface/diving lures included the famed Basser at ¾ oz., 4¼" length and the King Basser at 1⅛ oz., 5" length. The Dowagiac Minnow (150) was still in production with surface hardware and painted gold eyes weighing 1 oz., 3¾" long. The Baby Dowagiac was also still available in ½ oz., 2½" length. An old Heddon floating/diving standby is the Lucky 13 and it was available in a ⅝ oz., 4" version and the Baby Lucky 13 was ⅜ oz. and 2¾" long. The classic Meadow Mouse was ½ oz. and 2¾" long. The wooden Punkinseeds were no longer available but the Punkinseed Spook came in a ⅝ oz., 2⅛" version. This is one of Heddon's most collectible baits and comes in a variety of colors and eye patterns, making it fun to collect.

The River Runt was still available in wood at ½ oz., 2¾" length; however, the River Runt Spook had really supplanted interest in the lure by 1952. The River Runt Spook was available in standard ½ oz., 2½" length; Floating, ½ oz., 3" length; Midget, ⅜ oz., 2⅛" length; Midget Digit, ⅜ oz., 1⅝" length; Jointed Sinking, ⅝ oz., 2⅞"; and Jointed Floating, ¾ oz., 3⅞". The River Runt Spooks are very collectible and the color variations are great. River Runts with the gold or silver foil inserts are tough to find and make nice additions to a collection. Also, the lure originally came in two-piece hardware, and it also had box variations. By 1952, River Runts were in surface hardware and most had gold eyes. The Shad never had gold eyes and I have found some River Runts from boxes with 1948 catalogs with white eyes. New for 1952 was the introduction of the Tadpolly Spook and the wooden Tadpollys were no longer available. The Tadpolly Spook was a ⅜ oz., 3" lure that eventually was available in numerous additional sizes through the years. It was a phenomenal lure for salmon and became a favorite for Coho fishing in the Great Lakes.

The Tadpolly Spooks started with gold eyes, then no eyes, and eventually blush eyes. The Heddon Torpedo was a wooden lure weighing ¾ oz. and 4⅛" long, and was a nice collectible. The diving/floating Heddon Vamp was still available in wood in four models: the Vamp at ⅝ oz., 4½"; the Jointed Vamp at ¾ oz., 4¾"; the Giant Vamp at 1⅝ oz., 5½"; and the Giant Jointed Vamp at 1⅞ oz., 6¾". The Zig-Wag in wood was available as a ½ oz., 3¼" lure, and the King Zig-Wag for salmon fishing was available as a 1⅛ oz., 5" lure. Heddon had introduced the Vamp Spook in a rather unstable plastic in the 1930s but the Vamp Spook in 1952 was well made in Tenite 2 and weighed in at ¾ oz. and was 4¼" long. The Vamp Spook soon took over the Vamp line. Heddon also had some deep running lures, such as the Dowagiac Spook weighing ¾ oz., 3⅜" long. This plastic bait is highly desired by collectors and the lure came with gold eyes and an extended line tie in 1952, while early ones had glass eyes. Also, Black Shore (XBW) is a very rare color in this lure.

A wooden lure from this time was the Go Deeper Crab available in ½ oz., 3½" length and a deep diving lip. The River Runt Spook also had the Go Deeper versions available in ½ oz. and ⅝ oz. at 3⅛" and 3½" lengths. The Jointed Go Deeper River Runt Spook was ⅝ oz., 4¼" long. In addition to the above lures, Heddon made a complete line of fly rod baits, most in Spook versions, by 1952. They also made Stanley hooks that are collectible. With all of the variety offered by Heddon, it is easy to see the popularity of this company to collectors. Also, we Baby Boomers all remember the success of a Heddon Crazy Crawler, River Runt, or Meadow Mouse in filling our limits on Large Mouth Bass here in the Great Lakes region. Heddon was out of business as a separate entity by 1984, but the legend lives on through offerings by Pradco yet today. Heddon box history and many lures are detailed in 70 pages in my *Modern Fishing Lure Collectibles, Volume 1*.

Not common but a great find would be either of these decoys. The green perch is a "4-point" and the Rainbow is a "Batwing." $500.00 for 4-point in this condition, up to $1,200.00. Batwings sell for $1,500.00 – 4,000.00 usually, wooden tail models are at the high end of the scale.

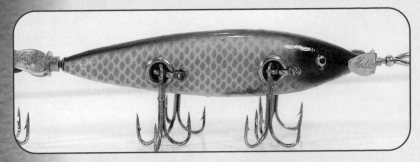

Seldom does one think of Heddon without thinking of its classic 150s such as this one. Most bring $125.00 – 250.00. Surface hardware models, $50.00 – 150.00. Many exceptions exist bringing $250.00 – 500.00 and early 1904 solid color models will bring thousands of dollars. One caution is to be aware of fakes and repainted solid colors, as it is simple to repaint a lure as a solid color.

Likely the most recognized Heddon bait is its River Runt Spook series of lures. This is one of the Dealer Dozens mentioned on page 23 for which I received $1,000.00 in late 2003. All of the boxes contained mint lures and 1947 – 1948 pocket catalogs. A few of the lures were two-piece hardware but most were surface. The red/silver/red Midget does not belong with these but I put it in to show it as an early 1950s rare foiled example. Dealer Dozen of new in box Runts: $1,000.00; Foiled River Runts from early 1950s, $50.00 – 75.00.

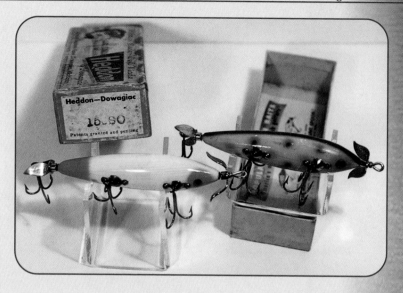

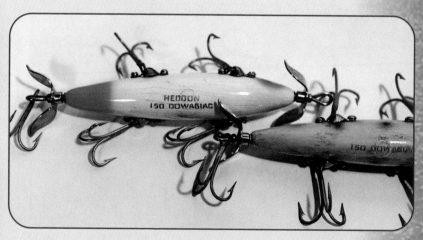

Two surface rig 150s from the late 1940s or early 1950s, sold online for a little over $200.00 to the same buyer in February 2004. The Spotted Orange model had the correct box, 150SO, and the r/w/r model did not have a box. These lures were in very good to excellent minus condition. The red/white one was very nice but just needed cleaning (age lines is all). The Spotted Orange had some minor pointers as shown. $75.00 – 125.00.

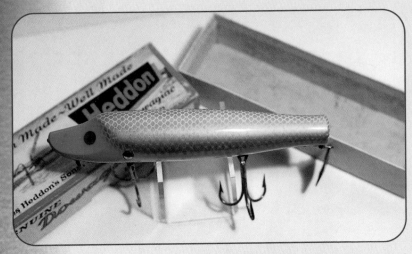

Heddon Flaptail in colorful Allen Stripey color. Model 7050PAS, painted eyes from late 1940s or early 1950s, with correct box, sold online in early 2004 for $65.00. Range is $50.00 – 100.00 for this lure from this time period.

Crab Wigglers are classic Heddon lures in high demand. This is an early one in a very early box, downward leaping bass on cover, with specific information about the lure on the side of the box. The lure has some light varnish loss but no paint loss and will bring a premium due to its early year and box type. $300.00 – 500.00.

Rare lure and box type: Heddon Bass Bug and early downward leaping two-piece cardboard box. $300.00+.

Two more difficult to find lures: River Runtie Spook for fly rods on right, and a Punkie Spook on the left with the treble hook. $125.00 – 250.00 each.

Typical of the 1940s and early 1950s, this shot shows two Punkinseed Spooks: a nice Meadow Mouse in wood and a wooden 2120 Crazy Crawler (introduced in 1940). $50.00 minimum to $125.00 for each of these lures, the Meadow Mouse being the most valuable. Most Punkinseed Spooks will sell for $75.00 – 125.00.

A closer view of the Mouse and 2120 with the addition of a 2100 wooden Crazy Crawler that is a little earlier. Note the three color eyes. $50.00 – 125.00.

Less valuable but new in 1952 is this member of the Tiny Trio by Heddon: Yellow Shore color Tiny River Runt Spook with gold eyes and gold lettering on belly in correct 1952 box. $20.00 – 30.00 as shown. Loose lures will only bring $10.00 – 15.00.

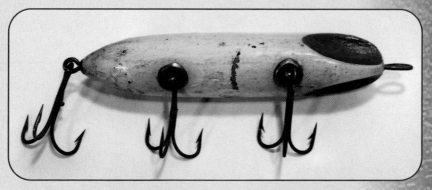

Very rare Heddon prototype of a Hastings or Moonlight type Wobbler made in 1906 – 1908 according to the Heddon expert Dale Roberts after he examined the brass cup hardware. Many companies toyed with copying other successful lures and then pulled them from the line if any lawsuits or litigation was pending. This was never put into production, however, it was clearly fished by the hook drag on the belly and the paint loss. Archival piece, no trade value known, but it would most likely bring $500.00+ if sold.

The belly side of an Artistic Minnow, another very early and very rare Heddon lure. Note the hand-painted gill marks and the single belly weight. Part of the gill marks were accidentally removed by using a "lemon cloth" polishing it. Be careful of hand-painted items such as this as the varnish is under the paint in some cases, such as the gill marks on this lure. These lures came with a lead weight in the same egg shape as the lure, and they are almost impossible to find. $300.00 – 500.00; more with weight.

Two lures any Heddon collector would want to own: a green crackle back Heddon 100, L-rig hardware, name on propellers, two hand-painted gill marks, and a Heddon 150 in a great color — Frog-scale. It also has name on propellers, L-rig and name on its belly. Heddon 100, $300.00+; Heddon 150, $1,200.00+ due to color.

My personal favorite Heddon 150, Model 151 (Rainbow color), excellent in box, L-rig, name on propellers, fat body with high forehead, 1915 – 1930 era. Rainbow is a premium color to collectors even though not exceptionally rare in Heddon lures. $500.00 – 1,200.00.

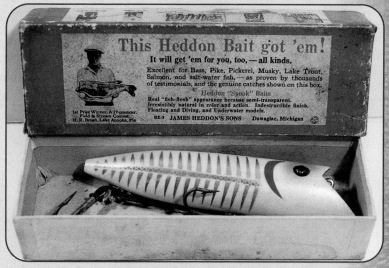

A Heddon King Basser, Model 8569 color PLXB in the famous Heddon "Brush Box." The box is named after Mr. Brush holding his 17-pound bass. It is common in the late 1930s and early 1940s prior to going to the upward leaping bass box for most lures and the Fish-Flesh boxes for spook lures. Also, the River Runt Spooks received their own boxes in the 1940s. The lure is not all that rare but is beautiful and was a heavy duty lure designed specifically because the hook hardware was being pulled out of the regular Basser lures by Salmon in the Pacific Northwest. $75.00 – 125.00.

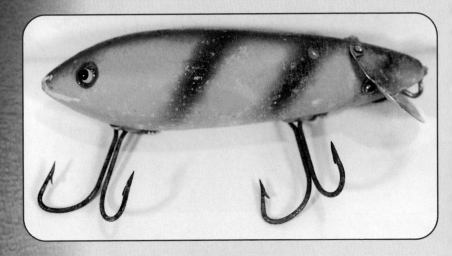

A Heddon Crab Wiggler in Bar Perch showing one of three diving lip varieties, sold online for $30.00+ in early 2004 in very good minus condition. $30.00 – 75.00.

The Big Six: Heddon

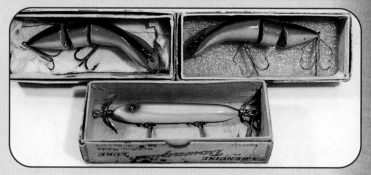

Three collectible lures: two Game Fishers in Rainbow, the one on the right with the hard-to-find weedless hooks. Also, a beautiful Torpedo Model 130 RB (Rainbow). The weedless hook Game Fisher is an early one in the Downward leaping bass box and both lures are L-rig hardware. The beautiful glass-eyed Torpedo is about mint but has the less desirable surface hardware, making it a little newer, but still valuable. $125.00 – 300.00 each.

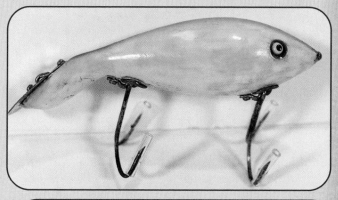

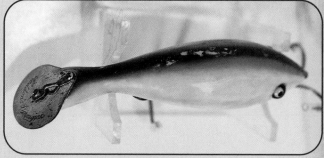

A Heddon Rainbow color Tadpolly with marked diving lip, single line tie, glass eyes, double hook variety, L-rig hardware, selling for $38.00 online in early 2004 in very good minus condition, but a nice color. $35.00 – 75.00 for most wooden Tadpollys except the earliest ones.

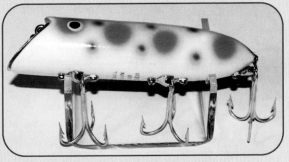

An example of one of Heddon's latest wooden lures from 1952, the rare Widget fly rod lure. These easily trade for $50.00 – 125.00.

Next in time for Heddon wooden lures was the reintroduction of a number of wooden lures in the 1960s called "Heddon Originals." Shown is a nice Strawberry Spot Basser from the 1960s in mint condition. This surface hardware, painted-eye lure had a metal plate on diving lip without a name. The very first Bassers were called Head-On Bassers for only two years. Then they were marked Heddon Basser, then not at all on the lips. Any of the lures marked "Original" come from this reintroduction time period. $35.00 – 50.00, maybe more with box.

America was invaded by the Finns in the early 1960s and their Rapala fishing lure won most of the battles, if not the war. Most companies responded and Heddon came out with the Heddon Wood Cobra in response to the very successful Rapala lure made of balsa. I normally fished Heddons and my tackle box in the 60s had at least a dozen of these lures. Collectors are just now catching on to the fact that they are not that common in mint condition. $10.00 – 15.00.

Pradco now owns the rights to Heddon lures and has marketed a couple of different series to capitalize on the great old wooden lures. The first was the Centennial Edition in 1994 and I have sold literally over a thousand of them. They made Wooden Zaragossas, Darting Zaras, Lucky 13s, and River Runts in this series. This photo shows two boxes. $25.00 – 45.00.

Perch Wooden River Runt shaped like the River Runt Spooks and not like the original River Runts. $25.00 – 45.00 boxed.

Heddon — Plastic Lures

Now we shift to the collectible Heddon plastics! As a group, there is not a hotter plastic lure collectible than Heddon's. I did show some in the previous chapter from the 1940s, but any of the Heddon plastics have a following, right up to the last ones in 1983 – 1984. The Heddon Preyfish from near the end of the company often trades for $100.00+ new in the box, to give you an idea. The thing to be aware of, however, is that Pradco still makes many plastic Heddon lures and these are of little to no collector value for the most part.

I recommend reading my *Volume 1*, Chapter One, on Heddons from the Modern Era (e.g. post-1940) for complete details. It gives a photo essay of box history, hundreds of photos and descriptions, and detailed pricing data within the text. Also, the newer versions of Luckey and White recognize the value and importance of Heddon plastic lures and show many illustrations. The lures are too numerous to name them all here, but always watch for: Punkinseeds, unusual colors in River Runts (foil inside for instance), Hi-Tails, any of the Spook fly rod baits, the rare Wee Tad fly rod lure from the 1980s, the Preyfish series of lures, Cracklebacks, Heddon Hedd Plugs, Vamp Spooks, and even the three eye colored Crazy Crawlers in plastic.

Better colors include brown and green crawdad from the late 1970s – 1980s, Black Shore in all but the River Runt where it is common, Yellow Shore in Punkinseeds, Red/White Shore in Punkinseeds, any non-catalog colors for any of the lures, naturalized fish patterns from the recent periods, etc. Many colors are very common such as red/white Sonics. This was one of the colors sold to wholesale houses so it is everywhere. The same was true for certain Punkinseed colors. So, a Shad is more unusual than a Bluegill in it.

This little field guide will not make one an expert on Heddon plastic lures, but it should at least make you feel a little more comfortable while out looking for lures. Hopefully, you will do a better job of recognizing common Heddons from the better ones.

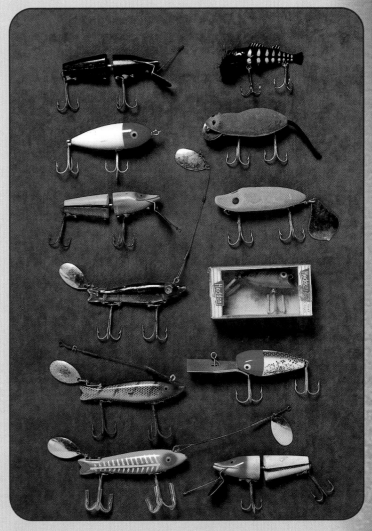

Heddon with one Bug-N-Bass; left row from top to bottom: Scissortail, Baby Zara, Scissortail, three Dowagiac Spooks; right row from top to bottom: Small Bug-N-Bass by Buckeye Baits, Heddon Mouse, small Flap-tail Mouse, Tiny Lucky 13, Deep 6, Scissortail. Dowagiac Spooks, $50.00+; Scissortails, $35.00+; Deep Six, $10.00 – 15.00; Baby Zara, $10.00; Flaptail Mouse, $75.00; and newer Mouse, $15.00 – 20.00. The non-Heddon Bug-N-Bass usually trades for $35.00 – 50.00.

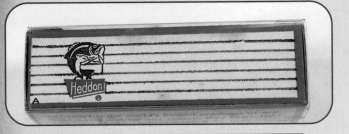

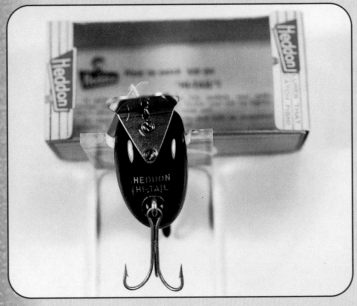

Details of a blue stripe box with new Hi-Tail, a short-run bait from the early 1960s. Note gold stencil on belly; often stencil coloring is a clue to dating Heddon lures. Hi-Tails bring high prices with a minimum of $50.00 new in the box for standard colors.

Black Shore Baby Zara Spook, 365 XBW, gold eyes, surface belly hardware, tail inverted bell hardware, in early 1950s cardboard box with a plastic top with upward bass logo. $35.00 – 50.00.

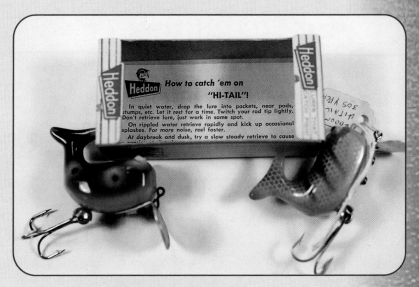

Two more Hi-Tails, frog and perch and a blue stripe box. This box type is the last before the Heddon-Daisy era began. $50.00 – 75.00 each, maybe even a little more with box.

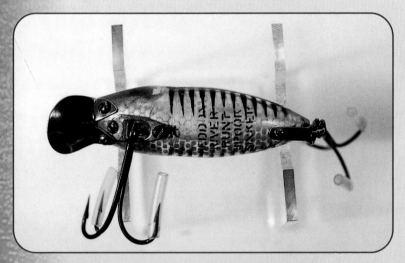

Photos show the details of a common color but early hardware type for a River Runt Spook. The two-piece, or flap-rig, hardware is prized by collectors as it pre-dates the surface hardware common by the late 1940s. But, keep in mind that early Tenite 1 models may be unstable due to problems with early plastics. All of the Tenite 1 models had this hardware. Most of the Tenite 2 models had surface rig but some of the early ones had this two-piece hardware. This is color XRS, Silver Shore, and is very common. $20.00+ due to early hardware. $10.00 in surface rig.

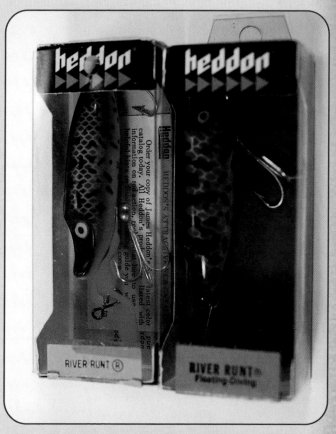

Two of some of the rare colors in recent models, a DD9400 GR and a 9400 BRS. Both of these trade fro $50.00 or more new in the sealed box. A recent GR Zara Spook sold for nearly $300.00 online in March of 2004. A GR Sonic sold or $700.00 new on card a few years ago. This is a hot color to be sure.

Two common Perch color River Runt Spooks. The top one is the more recent white eye, more green color. Note the gold eyes on the darker yellow perch on the bottom. These are very common colors in River Runts. $8.00 – 16.00 for surface, more for two-piece.

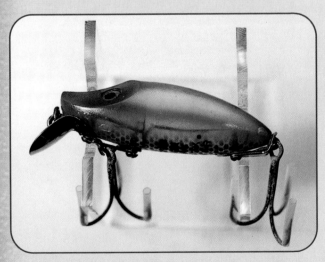

A better color and a two-piece Rainbow River Runt Spook. $40.00 – 60.00.

A very difficult to find and valuable "gold foil" Midget River Runt from the mid-1950s. This nice lure with gold eyes and surface hardware is worth $50.00+. I bought two of these at a lure show in April 2004 for $55.00 each, one silver foil, one gold.

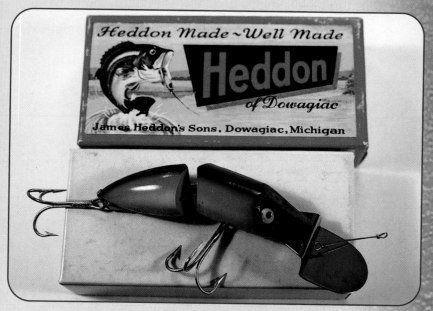

A mint in the upward bass box Jointed River Runt, Model D 9430-RB, in the gorgeous Rainbow pattern, my personal favorite. Note the gold eyes and surface hardware. Though not shown, the box is correctly labeled. Not all Runts came in the special box for River Runts, as can be seen by this example. I paid $75.00 for this combination from John Kolbeck in a private sale in 2000. $75.00 – 125.00 due to color and the fact that the box is a bass box.

Clockwise from top, the large wooden floating Model 740 in early two-piece hardware in Crappie; a common colored Sunfish, SUN, in the small plastic Model 380; the Model 730 smaller wooden sinker in tough to find Yellow Shore, XRY with surface belly hardware, and two-piece tail hardware; a standard color Crappie in the plastic Model 9630 CRA; and two examples of the Fly Rod Punkie Spook, one in Crappie and one in Bluegill. Punkie Spooks, $125.00 – 200.00; Wood Crappie, $75.00 – 150.00; Plastic Model 380 SUN, $50.00 – 75.00; Model 730 wooden XRY, $125.00 or more due to rare color; Model 9630 CRA recently sold for $98.00 new in box online in early 2004.

New in box 9630 XRY, surface hardware, gold eyes, black stenciling. $150.00 – 200.00 as XRY is relatively rare in Punkinseeds, even plastic ones.

Difficult to find 9630 XRW in gold eyes with surface hardware compared to a 9630 in Shad (SD) with yellow eyes and surface hardware. Both better lures with the Shad, $100.00+. XRW, $300.00+, as it is very rare.

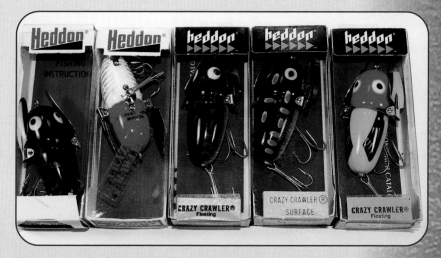

Five new-in-the-box 9120s. The Diamond boxes are all sealed. From left to right: 9120 BF in earliest black triangle Victor box; 9120 XRW in Victor box, white eyes with large black eyeballs; 9120 BF in sealed Victor Diamond box with no significant difference from earlier 9120 BF; 9120 PM in sealed Kidde Diamond box with yellow eyes and black eyeballs; and 9120 YRH in sealed Kidde Diamond box with white eyes and a smaller black eyeball than the earlier 9120 XRW. Of these, the 9120 PM is actually the hardest to find new in a sealed box. Even any of these relatively newer Crazy Crawlers are in high demand among collectors, especially boxed as this. $40.00+ each, general range would be $40.00 – 60.00, but rare colors will bring much more.

A very rare Tiny Torpedo in Silver Foil insert, not the introductory year but a tough bait to find, in a Daisy box. Most Torpedo Spooks do not bring much more than $8.00 – 12.00 each, but this one is hard to find with the foil insert in it. $50.00+ boxed.

An early Tadpolly Spook with gold eyes, black dots, next to a more recent version in Black Shore. Early gold eye from the 1950s, $16.00 – 22.00; 1980s XBW, $8.00.

An early Tiny Lucky 13 with gold eyes. The two little dots above the eye in gold are from the factory. This is one of the Tiny Trio introduced in 1952. $16.00 – 22.00 loose, more if boxed.

An early Perch Magnum Tiger next to a later Prowler; a Tiger; and a Tiger Cub (above) in a great color from the re-introduction in the 1980s. Prowlers trade for $12.00 – 20.00 and the Tigers bring over $20.00 loose. Add more if boxed.

The hard-to-find Commando. This short run vinyl type lure is quite rare, especially boxed. $16.00 – 30.00.

A desirable Crawshrimp. $50.00+.

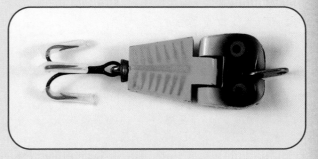

A Tiny Stingaree in Yellow Shore from the late 1960s with gold eyes. $22.00 – 35.00.

Display case of Sonics. A nice variety of Heddon Model 385s. Sonics normally trade for around $12.00 – 20.00 each, but rare colors such as the orange one in the center row are worth $100.00. Also, the Vibraflash lures located in center-three, second row from left, trade for $60.00+. The Gold Foil, third over on bottom from left, is a better lure, trading at $60.00+, and the red one is very rare, $100.00+. Right under the red one is a Baby Bass pattern that is very collectible, and though fairly common, commands $25.00+. The Perch, the red/white, the Shad, and most others are in the $12.00 – 20.00 range.

A White Coach Dog Firetail and a rarer colored Bar Fish Top Sonic. Overall, the Top Sonics are the toughest to locate. Bar Fish is a good color in any of the Sonics. Coach Dog Firetail, $20.00+; Top Sonics all trade for $35.00 – 50.00.

Rare Natural Fish/Bluegill in Ultra Sonic in a 1982/83 box. This is a rare type of Sonic (less common than Sonics and Super Sonics) and a very rare color pattern from a short run of lures. $100.00+.

A most difficult to find orange with black spots 385 Sonic and a nice Shad Top Sonic. This is a second type of orange Sonic. Note the difference in eye color and fin color. Sonic, $75.00 – 125.00; Top Sonic, $40.00 – 60.00.

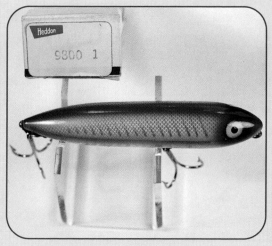

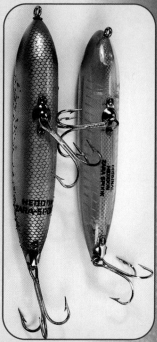

9250 SS Zara Spook in box with nose line tie, a 9250 Zara Spook with chin line tie in a 9800 Research Box, and the two lures compared. The older Zara is actually 4⁷⁄₁₆" long, surface hardware on tail and belly, Heddon and Zara-Spook are perpendicular to tail on belly, white eyes w/black pupils and black blush. The newer Zara is 4⁵⁄₁₆" long, surface tail and belly hardware. Original Heddon Zara Spook is parallel on belly toward center, eyes are more cream-colored with black pupils, and still has blush around eyes. Zara Spooks are very collectible but most collectors only want the early line tie at the end of the nose. Zara Spooks sell for $12.00 – 200.00+, depending on color, style, year, and with or without a box. The general range for Zaras is $12.00 – 40.00.

A new from its cardboard shipping box Sonic Kit SK-4, four common colors, black stenciling, yellow eyes, and black pupils. $80.00 – 100.00, as kits are harder to find. Each lure is worth about $12.00 – 15.00 if loose due to being common colors.

Older gold eye Chugger in top photo and newer Chugger in bottom photo. Chuggers are very collectible but the old gold eyes are preferred. Older yellow, $40.00+ in box; white, $16.00 – 22.00 loose.

Model 550 NB Preyfish. $75.00+.

Large Crackleback, Model 8050 in orange. $40.00 – 60.00.

Frog Spot Brush Popper with spinner. $40.00 – 60.00. Rare color Brush Poppers have sold for up to $175.00.

Perch Hedd-Hunter 9305, Medium Diver. $20.00 – 100.00+, depending on color. This one is common and on the low end of the range.

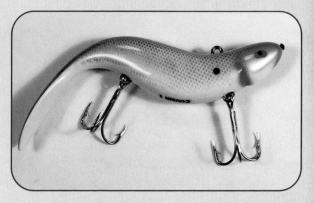

Heddon's First Cousin, Cousin I, floater. $20.00 – 30.00.

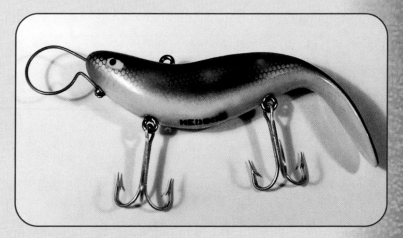

Heddon's Second Cousin, Cousin II, sinker. $20.00 – 30.00.

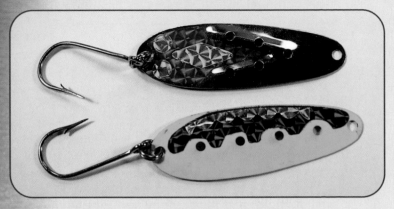

Believe it or not, two tough to find Heddons. Top one is a Sculpin, bottom one is the Sounder. Flutter spoons introduced in the 1980s. $10.00 each, as recent metal lures are not in high demand.

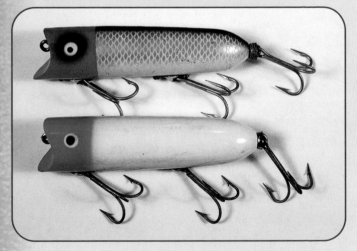

Lucky 13s are not as collectible as many Heddon lures as they made so many, but the earlier ones such as the PRH color on top is a better lure than the newer R/W without blush around its eyes. PRH, $15.00 – 20.00; R/W, $8.00 – 12.00.

Three <...> ht: 2500 JRH, BB (both better colors), and L <...> boxes, BB in Kidde box. The JRH and BB wo <...> new in box, and the Perch only about $20.00 <...>

Introductory box for Deep 6, early 1960s, Model 345 Y. $20.00 – 35.00 in this early box.

Left to right: Model 370 Tiny Lucky 13 Frog Scale, JRH, inverted bell hardware in one-piece Daisy box; 2400 JRH, Baby Lucky 13 in slide-top Victor Comptometer box; 2400 BRS (rare color) in Victor Recreation box; 2400 PRH (good color); 2400 BB (good color), both in Kidde boxes. Any of these would bring $40.00+, as they are good colors and new in boxes.

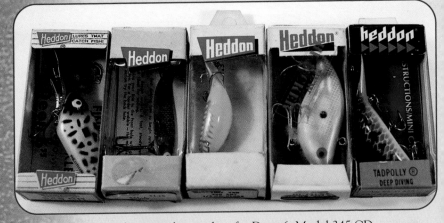

Left to right: Another introductory box for Deep 6, Model 345 CD; a common lure in a nice box, Sonar 431 L in one-piece Daisy box with fishing instructions, price $1.15 on end label; a Yellow Shore Tiny Tad Model 390 XRY in Daisy-Heddon box from Rogers, Arkansas; a very hard-to-find lure, the short-lived Heddon Hi-Jacker, Model 9355 SSD, ⅜ oz. size in a Victor transitional box, marked New Hi-Jacker on box top; a rare color Tadpolly 9000 in BRS in a Victor Recreation box. Deep-Six, $20.00 – 35.00; Sonar, $10.00; Tadpolly Spook in Yellow Shore, $20.00 – 30.00; Hi-Jacker, $25.00 – 35.00; and BRS Tadpolly, $35.00 – 60.00.

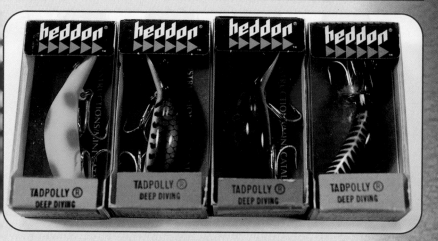

A family of Tadpolly 9000s, from left to right: FYR; BB; BF; and XBW, the first three in Kidde boxes, the last one in the last box made with James Heddon's Sons only on left side of box. The FYR and BB would bring $30.00+ while the other two would bring $20.00 – 30.00. The FYR may bring up to $50.00, as it is a rare color.

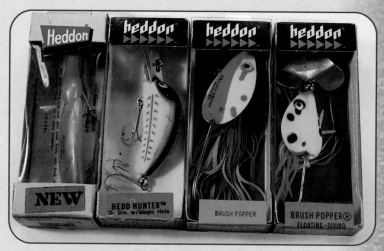

These are all better lures to find. An introductory box for the Commando Model 2020 RWS in Daisy one-piece box; a nice color Hedd-Hunter Model 9320 YFO with rattle, ⅜ oz. Class; a Brush Popper with a small propeller instead of a large normal one in Model 5440 RFY, ½ oz. Class in Victor Recreation box; and a Brush Popper with normal propeller in Model 5430 CDF, ¼ oz. Class in a Kidde box. These are all better lures. $50.00 – 175.00 for some Brush Poppers. Also the YFO Hedd-Hunter is a great and fairly rare color.

Two pre-1970 Spin Fins shown upside down to read the spinner blades. These are attractive but not in too much demand yet. $5.00 – 10.00 each.

Two shots of Prototype Hedd-Hunter type lure made of wood with rear Heddon marked propeller. Archival piece, no trade value. $500.00+ if for sale.

The last Heddon wooden lure introduced, a Model X100, Sun B5 Timber Rattler in a transitional Ebsco, Inc. package. This white cedar lure is not seen too often. Also, a close-up of the lure itself, 2½" long, large glass eyes, surface belly hardware, simple screw tail hardware, Heddon on belly in black letters. These are normaly trading for $18.00 – 24.00.

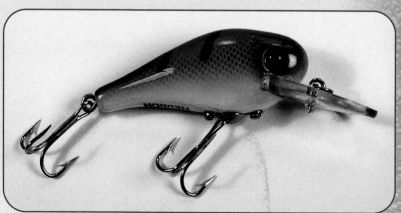

Midget River Runt showing the two-piece hardware used on many lures prior to switching to the surface rig in the 1940s on most lures. XBW is a common color in this lure but the earlier hardware and excellent condition make it valued at $18.00 – 24.00.

Baby Chugger 9522 NPY, ³⁄₈ oz. lure taken new from its Daisy/Heddon box for this photo. This is a rare color in a highly desired lure. $125.00+ new in box.

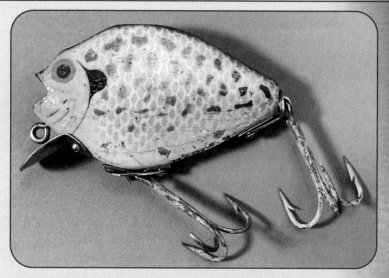

Early Punkinseed 740 in rougher shape showing two-piece hardware and line tie under chin. Sold online in 2004 for $47.00 in good plus condition.

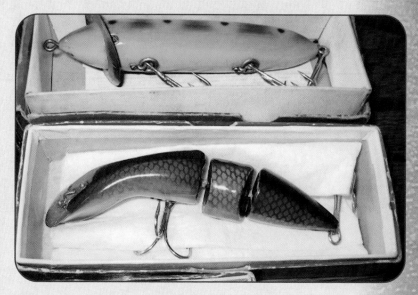

Two pretty examples of collectible Heddon lures in two-piece boxes. The top lure is the beautiful L-rig 200 in frog and below is the green scale Game Fisher. The 200 is valued at $300.00 – 500.00 in downward leaping bass box. The Game Fisher is in a common color but in a nice box, so it is valued at $125.00+.

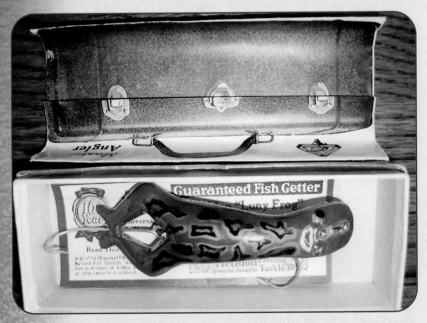

A screaming mint Luny Frog with the rare tackle box catalog insert in box. $200.00 – 300.00.

Paw Paw

I became a "serious collector," not just an accumulator of lures, about ten years ago. When I started trading with others I found a general disdain for Paw Paw lures with only one in a hundred interested in them. Today, this has gone full circle so most are interested in Paw Paw and most certainly appreciate the variety of lures offered by this Paw Paw, Michigan company. I believe this is because unlike the other big six companies, Paw Paw did not produce catalogs for the public (trade catalogs and wholesale fliers, yes) so it has been harder for the general collector to nail down its offerings.

I published the first complete set of Paw Paw color catalog sheets in any modern lure book a few years ago. Since then, and even before, more and more people are seriously collecting these nice lures, both the wooden and the plastic ones. Paw Paw has come of age and taken its place in collecting history just as it did in lure production history.

Paw Paw bought out the former Moonlight Baits and eventually purchased Arnold Lures as well. Today the lure rights are owned by Shakespeare but the last lures produced under the Paw Paw banner were the short production, but collectible, wooden and plastic lures of the mid-1970s produced by Shakespeare, primarily in Hong Kong. Actually, some of these lures sell for decent money and are very beautiful indeed.

Collectors are very interested in many Paw Paw lures and one will soon find out that many are identifiable by the diving lip and hardware types. Certain color patterns are also typical for this company, as is true for most companies. As to rare color patterns, the Rainbow Trout pattern is fairly hard to find on the Caster lures, and the Gantron colors are outstanding. The most common colors are the Pikie colors and the Green Scale that is very common indeed.

Spinning lures were added in a number of the same lures in the early 1950s and eventually most of Paw Paw's standard lures were available in the lighter sizes for spinning. By 1960, Paw Paw listed 11 new lures for spinning: Pikaroon, Jointed Pikaroon, Spinning Torpedo, Spinning Wounded Minnow, Little Jigger, The Jig-a-Lure, Fuzzy Mouse, Feather Midget, The Midget Lure, Spinning Plunker, and the Old Faithful. Most of these lures were very similar to competitive offerings from Creek Chub, Heddon, and Shakespeare. They also made a Spinning Top-Eye, Spinning Sunfish, and Spinning Swimming Mouse. Their new line of Bonehead lures had many spinning lure weights available. They even made a "Brilliant Bass Seeker" nearly identical to an L & S Bass-Master lure. Their Darter and Jointed Darter are very similar to the Creek Chub lures. And the list grows through time with more and more Paw Paw lures being offered in spinning weights.

Paw Paw made very few old metal lures and any of the marked spoons from the early period of the 1930s – 1940s are prized. The recent spoon offerings of the 1960s would not be valued more than most metal lures at $5.00 – 10.00 each. In addition to the lures already mentioned, the company had an extensive line of fly rod baits and natural baits in rubber for fly rod use.

Paw Paw bought out Moonlight Baits, an early producer of wooden baitcasting lures, and this gave the company a great line of lures on which to build. Paw Paw made many classic lures worth collecting including: its large hair mice, regular wooden mice in two different versions, the classic Bullhead lure, numerous wooden Wobblers, Old Flatside, an injured minnow, the Aristocrat Shiners in at least two sizes, Plunkers, underwater sinking Torpedo types, fat little underwater lures similar to Shakespeare Pumpkinseeds, and numerous River Runt type lures. Some of the most sought after of Paw Paw lures are the Caster series of lures, wooden lures in the shape of fish. I sold a Pike Caster in 2003 for $179.00, and that is not unusual. Add to the above many collectible Moonlight lures such as the Bass Seeker, the Crawfish, the Dreadnought, Floating Bait, Pikaroon, Jointed Pikaroon, Polly-Wag, Torpedo, Weedless, Ladybug Wiggler, Wobbler, Woodpecker, and Zig-Zag, and one gets an idea of the many lures available.

In addition to the ones already mentioned, Paw Paw also made a beautiful three-hook underwater minnow similar to a Heddon 100, a series of lures for Florida called the Bonehead lures, the ever popular Wotta-Frog, a Platypus, the Plenty Sparkle baits with rhinestones, Pikie Getum lures, Surf-Oreno type lures, and the Weedless Wow. By 1950, Paw Paw also made a complete series of lures in Tenite 2 including some in ⅜ oz. size for spinning. And, last but not least, do not forget the heavy duty hardware on a Flap Jack or its close cousin Crazy Mike, two early Tenite lures in the shape of a Flatfish that are trading for $20.00 – 50.00 each now.

So, if one finds a lure that is not marked and it looks similar to a Heddon, a Creek Chub, or a Shakespeare, it may be a Paw Paw. The Heddon Lucky 13 becomes Mister 13 for Paw Paw and the Heddon Chugger becomes The Lucky Popper. The Bass-Oreno and Babe-Oreno become the 4400 and 4200 Series. The Pumpkinseed by Shakespeare is very similar to a Sunfish by Paw Paw. Clearly the Moonlight era and early Paw Paw also gave us many original baits such as the Caster series and Wotta-Frogs. Many Paw Paw lures are marked on the diving lip. The paint on Paw Paw lures is gorgeous if the lures are in excellent shape, but one does notice varnish to be lacking on many and this leads to chipping and pointers if found in tackle boxes. Age lines are also more noticeable on Paw Paw lures as a general rule. But, some of the colors were outstanding and a Pikie Getum is a beautiful lure. The unusual Gantron colors in almost what I would call a "baby" shade are some of the prettiest lures ever.

The days of all Paw Paw lures being valued at $8.00 – 12.00 are long gone. Many of the better Paw Paw lures break the $100.00 mark regularly with such lures as the Bullhead, many of the Caster Series, and Wotta-Frogs. But even rare Plunker colors will bring $150.00 or more and the three-hook minnows are in the $150.00 – 400.00 range if excellent or better. In general, the pricing is indeed still lower as many people cannot identify the lures or simply do not know their importance. But, of the big six, this company has had the most dramatic growth in collector interest in the past five years, that much is certain. Bargains still exist, especially at auctions and in the field. Collectors with knowledge are going to be asking more for Paw Paw lures in the future.

Paw Paw box for its line of "Lucky Lures." I usually refrain from using the word "mint," but this box and lure are mint. Found in an antique shop in Pacific Grove, California, recently. Model 9301 J, 3¼" long, tack eyes. $50.00+.

The red version of the Lucky Lures box with a 3¾" green shiner scale, tack-eyed Paw Paw Pikie, not in the same shape, but nice. One thing that hurts these lures is the absence of paint on either of the eyes, so always look for that when buying a Paw Paw. This set is worth about $35.00.

The black and yellow box is the last one used by Paw Paw, and Shakespeare used a similar one as shown in the Shakespeare section. The other box is the common slide-top box with an arrowhead from the 1950s. $10.00.

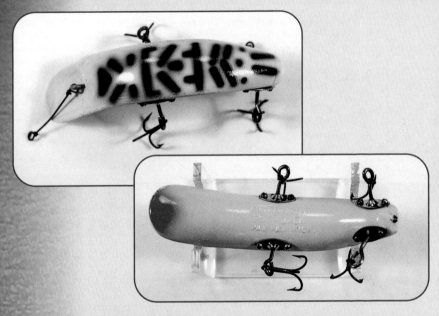

A nice early Aztec pattern Tenite Flap Jack, two views. This lure was made in Tenite as early as 1941 by Paw Paw. It is 3⅝" long, has hook hardware unique to the Flap Jack lures, and a plate with two little blade screws holding each hook hanger onto the lure body. The bottom has cast into the Tenite, "Paw Paw Bait Co. Flap Jack, Paw Paw, Mich." I paid $30.00+ for this on eBay in May of 2001.

A 2" Paw Paw spinner bait with no paint on eyes, painted cup hardware, and the smallest of its wooden Plunkers, 2¼" long, painted cup hardware, tack eyes. The little spinner baits are getting hot, and the Plunkers have always been in demand, though not as much as with Creek Chub Plunkers. Top bait worth $10.00 – 15.00 without paint on eyes; Plunker should fetch $20.00 or more.

A parade of Paw Paw Rainbows: a nice wooden 3" tack eye Plunker; a 3" tack eye surface bait similar to a Surf-Oreno, one spinner, narrower body; a River Runt type with tack eyes, 2½" long, simple screw tail hardware, pin in nose, screw line tie, showing the typical Paw Paw front hook hanger in the last photo. Any of the Rainbows are desirable and would bring $30.00+ depending on model.

An older, 2⅜" long Paw Paw wooden mouse that lost its tail, otherwise in fine shape, and a fuzzy brown Mouse, black stripe on back, leather tail, 2¼", to show hook hanger and box again, new in slide-top box without a model number. Either of these mice is collectible and would bring $30.00 or more.

One of the more collectible older Paw Paw baits, one of its Pike Casters in Pikie color, 5" long, typical Paw Paw front hook hanger, painted cup center hardware, simple screw tail hardware, back of lip marked Paw Paw. This one has a couple of small pointers and a little loss of paint on the tail but should command $40.00 or better. These are in demand.

The smaller of the Wotta-Frogs in a yellowish green tone, 2⅞". These are also still growing in popularity, and I have not sold one for less than $50.00 in three years.

A J.C. Higgins brand Injured Minnow (made for Sears) made by Paw Paw, as nice as they come. This was found new in the wrong box. Tack eyes, painted cup hardware, 3¾" long, wooden lure. In this shape, it should bring $40.00 or more.

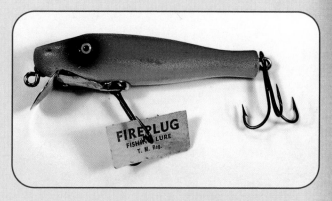

The Paw Paw version of a Fireplug Pikie, 3¼" long, Paw Paw cup front hardware, painted screw/washer tail hardware, tack eyes, great shape except for the little black mark seen, just a little dirty but cannot be cleaned easily either. As with all fire lacquer lures, this is a premium item, $75.00+.

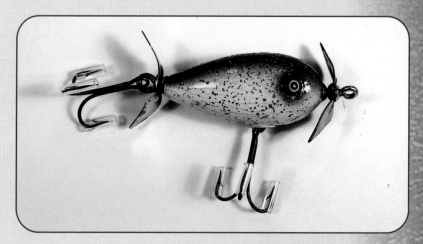

The little Sunfish lure is in far better shape than the one shown earlier. This is model 1312 and should bring $30.00.

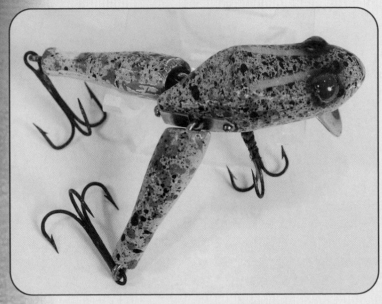

One of the most collectible of the Paw Paw lures is the Wotta-Frog made in three sizes and yellow splatter and green splatter colors. This is the large size and sold online in March 2004 for about $80.00 in very good plus condition. $60.00 – 90.00.

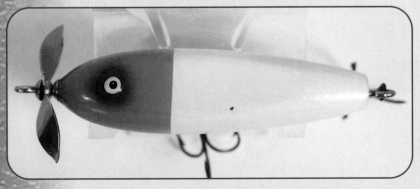

Another recent sale was this Old Flatside Injured Minnow type. Note the tack eye common of many of the lures. Sold for $28.00 online in 2004.

This more common type of Injured Minnow shows the painted cups typical of Paw Paw and the fact that the eyes on its Injured Minnow lures are on top of the head. Creek Chub versions have eyes on the sides. This lure is in rough shape but still sold for $12.00+ due to frog color.

Two size versions of the Aristocrat Shiner wooden lure designed for Florida. These lures were also made by Shakespeare and reintroduced under the Shakespeare/Paw Paw label of the mid-1970s. These two are the earlier models. In a 1959 wholesale catalog they were called Aristocrat Shiners. Earlier they were simply the Shiner and the Little Shiner. In 2004 these sold online for $12.00 – 18.00 each. The small was very good plus and the large one was very good minus.

Three examples of the Wobbler type lures that sometimes were named and sometimes were numbered by Paw Paw. The red/white is very common but these three and five others sold well online for me. $8.00 – 14.00 each. They will exceed $20.00 if mint and a nice color.

The wooden runt type lures were called Lippy Joe by Paw Paw and here are two examples showing two lip types. The green scale has the unmarked lip similar to one of the Shur-Strike lip styles and the bar scale has the standard diving lip/front cup combination of Paw Paw, most of which are marked. Depending on color and condition, range is $8.00 – 40.00. The green scale shown sold for $16.00 and the other I would value at $12.00 – 15.00, as the color is nice even with a little paint damage.

This view of a standard Pikie shows the traditional lip well. The lure has some paint loss, especially on the eye, which is common. Paw Paw made this style Pikie and the Pikie-Getum with a groove on each side of the mouth. The Pikie-Getum is worth more as it is older and less common. $8.00 – 20.00.

A surface bait in Frog by Paw Paw. This is an uncatalogued model without any spinners of which I have found about five examples. It is more slender than the Surf-Oreno or Paw Paw's surface types with spinners shown next. But, it is a Paw Paw lure. The Frog shown would only sell for $12.00 – 20.00 due to paint loss on back as shown. However, most of these lures should range from $12.00 – 40.00.

The small Surf-Oreno type lure by Paw Paw, also in Frog. Note the tack eye, painted cup, and propeller type. Also note the rear hook hanger is identical to the one on the green scale shown earlier. $30.00 – 40.00.

Actually this is a Moonlight Plunker. The dark red to black back shading is a typical Moonlight paint job. $30.00+.

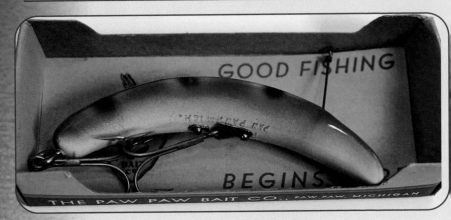

These four photos show details of a beautiful Crazy Mike from the late 1940s or early 1950s. This is similar to the Tenite Flap Jack with two hook gangs instead of the two trebles as on this lure. The Flap Jack was made as early as 1941 in Tenite and the Crazy Mike shortly followed. Early Flap Jack and Crazy Mike lures sell for $25.00 – 40.00 loose, and this would bring $65.00+ because it's boxed and a Frog.

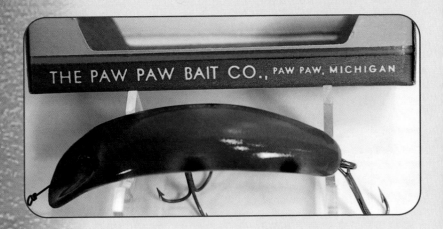

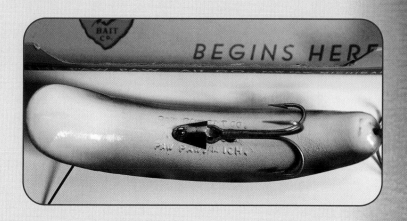

Pflueger (Enterprise Mfg.)

There is no dispute that Pflueger is the oldest of all of the big six companies, dating to the mid-1800s, and the company is famous for its terminal tackle and eventually rods and reels. However, like the other companies the vintage lure making did not begin until the late 1800s and early 1900s. Pflueger (and Four Brothers brand) did make a number of early collectible metal baits and some are very rare and valued highly. I traded one Maybug spinner for a few thousand dollars worth of Heddon plastics in 1995 as one example. Of course the Heddon plastics were not valued that high at the time but we still figured a value of nearly $2,000.00 on a metal lure in the trade.

This is an exception and not the rule. Most Pflueger metal goes for less than $20.00 an item, a lot of lures for less than $10.00, and many less than $5.00. But, there indeed are some nice ones being traded bringing $20.00+. Pflueger started making vintage lures for trolling and baitcasting in hard rubber, such as the Muskellunge Minnow shown in this section. This was a bait from the mid-1890s and is very rare in good shape. Many similar lures were made at the time by Pflueger.

The company made wooden minnows about the same time as James Heddon started, around 1901 and beyond. The earliest Pflueger minnows had see-through clip hardware that was similar to the Rhode's design, owned by Shakespeare. Shakespeare sued and won and Pflueger had to change its hardware system. So, if you have a five-hook minnow with see-through hardware, you have an early one. Pflueger came out with its famous "Never-Fail" hardware, a spiraling hook hanger on a disk inserted into the cup. It did not live up to its name and would indeed bend under severe pulling by large fish.

But, Pflueger Never Fail and the early Monarck Minnows are very collectible and would lead the list of desired baits more than likely. As an owner of the Muskellunge Minnow I can attest to its beauty, even though it does not photograph as well as lighter colored lures. However, most lure collectors still prefer wooden baits over all others and this keeps the prices down on some early rubber baits such as the Muskellunge Minnow and the early Shakespeare Evolution baits such as is shown on the front cover.

Collectors need to know that Pflueger switched from glass eyes to carved eyes earlier than most other companies, in the late 1930s. Also, likely due to the problems with Never Fail hardware, Pflueger added a strong surface rig hardware fairly early as well. So, just because it has carved eyes and surface rig does not mean that it is from the late 1940s or early 1950s. It could be an earlier one. Frankly, I think the Pflueger carved eye lures are beautiful anyway.

Pflueger became a leader in reel production with its top-of-the-line Pflueger Supreme baitcaster leading the way. The company made dozens of models and one can see them all in catalog reproductions in my *Volume 2*. The Supreme sold for $25.00 – 35.00 in the 1930s and 1940s, and it is no wonder it is collectible today. It is a great reel and one I fished with as a youngster. As a young man, the first two reels I purchased were the Pflueger Medalist 1495 for fly fishing (on my Heddon Pal glass rod), and a baitcaster.

I only mention the reels as it explains what happened to Pflueger with the lure lines. Enterprise Manufacturing, Pflueger's originator, always concentrated on terminal tackle and metal baits. This continued until Shakespeare purchased Pflueger in 1960. Four Brothers was the reel making division of Enterprise Manufacturing and the Pflueger reel line became its mainstay (early reels are marked Four Brothers) through the 1930s until closing in 1960. During this time period, Pflueger put more marketing and development efforts into the terminal tackle and reel components of its business than the lure making component. Lures were made and marketed but were never a central focus of the company, compared to Heddon or Creek Chub. In other words, Heddon and Creek Chub were examples of lure companies that produced reels, and Pflueger was a reel company that made some lures.

Pflueger did indeed make some fine early lures and continued to market a significant number of collectible baits right up into the 1950s. It even added a few before it became part of Shakespeare in 1960. The Cotton Cordell lure called the Gay Blade was first a Pflueger and is now owned by Pradco! This is how many lures evolve and actually change ownership. The Gay Blade (small metal sonic bait) and the Jerk Bait (Zaragossa type) were two of Pflueger's last offerings. Some of the most in demand are indeed its minnows, either see-through clip or Never Fail models. The Frug is another recent offering that has become hot lately, selling for $20.00 – 50.00 for a new in box plastic bait.

One could spend a lifetime just collecting the wide variety of Pflueger spinners, spoons, and related baits. Pflueger is the oldest of the big six companies and marketed terminal tackle since its beginning, including some of the most beautiful hammered spoon examples ever made during the 1800s. Most Pflueger lures are marked, even the smallest tandem spinner or miniscule Colorado blade. Not all, but most. The variety is endless as to size and design, and Pflueger made its famed Breakless Devon in a spinning size by 1952. Pflueger spoons included the Chum, Imperial, Last Word, Limper, Multilite, Rainbow Pearl, Record, Salamo, Scamper, Seattle Trout, and Self-Striker. Pflueger specifically made the Chum in spinning size and so marketed it in major trade magazines. The famed Tandem spinners were also available in spinning sizes. The Whoopee Spinner was a dressed single hook casting bait in the Al Foss design tradition. Other weighted spinners included the Snapie and the Zam spinners, weighted casting baits.

In addition to all of the baits I just mentioned still being produced in 1952, Pflueger offered the Globe Bait in three sizes, ⅝ oz., 2¾", ¾ oz., 3⅝", and 1⅓ oz., 5¼" for Muskie fishing. The Livewire Minnow is an attractive torpedo-shaped diving minnow that was in ¾ oz., 3¾" length in 1952. One of the most successful and most attractive of the Pflueger baits was the Mustang Minnow and it was available in 1952 in three sizes, ½ oz., 2¾", ⅝ oz., 4¼" and 1½ oz., 5" for Muskie fishing. Another highly prized Pflueger lure is the Pal-O-Mine and it was available in three sizes in 1952 and in a jointed version as well. The weights were ⅓ oz., ½ oz., and ¾ oz. in 2¾", 3¼", and 4¼" lengths. The Jointed Pal-O-Mine was available in the ½ oz. and ¾ oz. sizes only. A nice surface popper called the Poprite Minnow was available in ½ oz. and ⅝ oz. sizes at 3" and 4" lengths. It actually could be classed as a diving lure as it would dive upon fast retrieve like a Bass-Oreno. The Scoop Minnow (injured minnow type with front and rear propellers) was a true surface lure and came in ½ oz., 3" and ¾ oz., 3⅝" sizes in 1952. One of the oldest offerings was still available in the form of the Neverfail Minnow with front and rear propellers, three hooks, and carved eyes. All of the three-hook and five-hook minnows are desired by collectors, but I must admit that I think the carved eye Neverfail Minnows are as pretty as they come! See *Modern Fishing Lure Collectibles, Volume 1*, and the following pages for lure examples, and *Modern Fishing Lure Collectibles, Volume 2*, for all of the reels made by Pflueger.

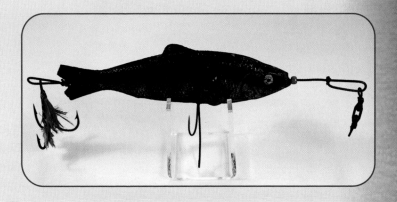

1890s Muskellunge Minnow from author's collection. This hard rubber, 7" Muskie bait does not photograph too well but it has brilliant hand-painted gill marks and the old lead based paint is still gorgeous. The only flaw is the chipping to tail common on these lures, but this is still one of the best ones around according to most collectors. It is very rare. $2,000.00 – 4,000.00.

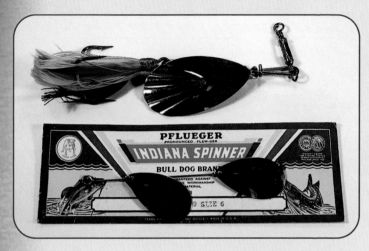

Older Pflueger spinner and a fairly common Model No. 599, Size 6, Indiana Spinner new on the card. Bulldog brand logo is older version of these. $15.00 each.

The Pflueger carved eye on a nice rainbow Pal-O-Mine, 4½" Model 5073, new from a plastic top cardboard box. $30.00 in this condition, $50.00+ with the box.

Pal-O-Mine in nice Pflueger color, smaller 3¼" version. Sold online in 2002 for $18.00.

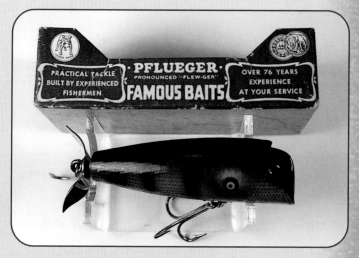

A new from the plastic slide-top box Poprite, similar to a Plunker. Carved eye Model 8500 in Natural Perch Scale, size 3 (3"). $30.00 – 40.00.

Spinning size Baby Scoop in silver flash. $20.00 – 30.00.

A plastic Scoop in black/white scramble finish, 2¾", cup hardware on belly, unmarked propellers. $15.00 – 20.00.

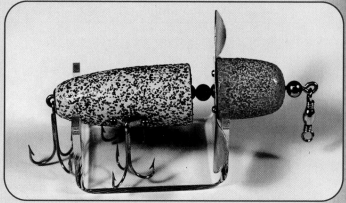

A copy of a Pflueger globe found mainly in the upper peninsula of Michigan and northern Wisconsin, made in the 1970s after Pflueger quit making them. $40.00+ is common for this lure. Globes sell for $40.00 – 125.00, or more if new in box.

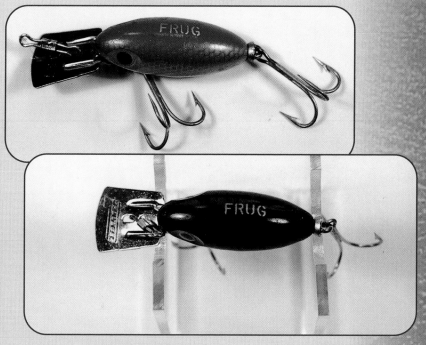

Two examples of one of the more collectible recent Pflueger baits, the Frug. Note the modernized trademark on the diving lip. Carved eyes, 1¾" long, inverted bell tail hardware, diving plane serves as front hook hanger. Early 2004 sales of Frug lures were $20.00 – 40.00 each for new in box examples.

Pflueger five-hook minnow with Neverfail hardware. $300.00 – 500.00.

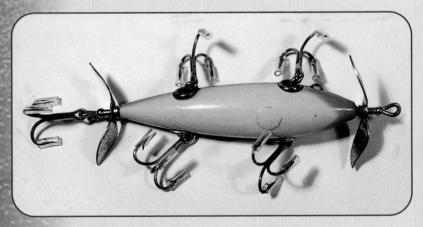

Bottom of five-hook minnow shown above. "PFLUEGER" is stamped on front prop only. $300.00 – 500.00.

An early "canoe" box by Pflueger. Box alone, $15.00 – 20.00 in excellent shape; more for rare lures.

The two-piece box after Pflueger went to a "modern" logo for a good lure, the Monarch Minnow (a three-hook minnow). $20.00 or better for a Minnow box, but in general, $10.00 for this box.

This old Pflueger Minnow sold online for nearly $40.00 even though in rough shape, paint loss on head, hook drag, and repaired years ago by its owner. The color is nice and it was an early lure. In good condition it would have brought much more. $200.00+ in excellent condition.

This wooden Wizard in baitcasting size is a classic collectible and found its way to Japan for $60.00+ selling online in 2004. $50.00 – 100.00.

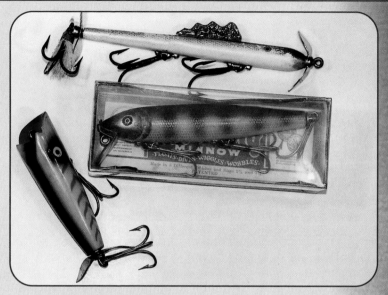

A grouping of collectible Pflueger lures including the Livewire on top, a carved eye minnow with typical Pflueger diving lip in box with plastic top (1950s) and a large sized Pop-Rite wooden popper also with carved eyes. Livewire, $60.00 – 100.00; Mustang Minnow, $50.00 – 75.00; and Pop-Rite, $40.00 – 50.00.

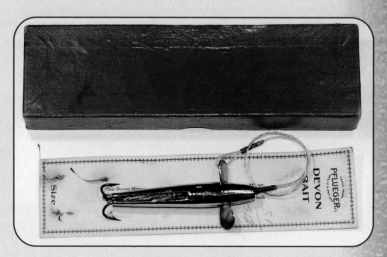

An older Pflueger piece is this early Breakless Devon, new on card and in box. This fine piece would likely trade for $125.00 – 200.00 even though metal as it is early, carded, and boxed. Breakless Devons without boxes trade in the $40.00 – 60.00 range commonly.

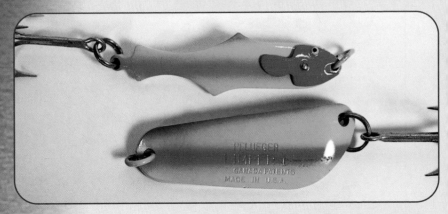

Two beautiful Rainbow metal Pflueger lures. The bottom one is a Limper-1, 1¹¹⁄₁₆" long. The top one is a Pippin Wobbler, 1¾" long counting tail hanger. It is not a fly rod Pippin, it is heavier for ultra light or weighted casting use. Either would sell for $30.00 or more due to mint quality and the color.

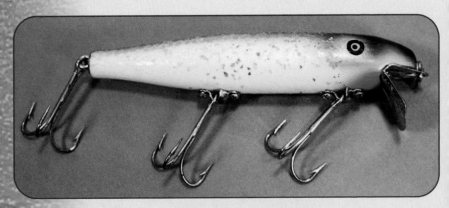

Silver Flash Pal-O-Mine, carved eyes, excellent condition. Sold online 2004 for $22.00.

Muskie size Mustang Minnow, note plates on back and belly. Carved eyes, heavy reinforced hardware, rust stain on wood but in decent shape elsewhere. Sold online in 2004 for $38.00.

Shakespeare

Of all of the lure companies, this one was closest to my home while growing up and it was often I visited its home town of Kalamazoo, Michigan, to see relatives living there. Shakespeare was a household word in our part of the world and it became one nearly everywhere fishing was popular due to its Wonderods and Wondereels of the 1950s.

But, Shakespeare also made many fine lures from its beginning until it began concentrating on primarily reel and rod production in the 1950s. Today it is a very large company headquartered in South Carolina and still produces rods, reels, and terminal tackle but not lures. Its last crack at lure sales was in the mid-1970s with the production of some fine traditional Shakespeare and Paw Paw lines, as it owned Paw Paw at the time. I have sold some of these rare 1970s wooden and plastic baits for upwards of $40.00 each, so some will be shown in this section.

But, some of the most expensive lures made by Shakespeare come early, very early, e.g. pre-1915. I once found a Rhodes Frog new in the cardboard box from about that time period. I sold it for $1,500.00. It then sold at Lang's Lure Auction later that year for $4,000.00. I still have a Rhode's frog but not new in the box that is rare indeed. Rhode's is a name that Shakespeare acquired from Mr. Rhode's when he sold his patented hook hanger system of a see-through clip to Shakespeare. This is the same one they sued Pflueger over and won. If you have a see-through it may be an early Shakespeare. Any of the early Rhode's or Shakespeare minnows will bring hundreds of dollars if in decent condition. I have sold or traded a few for over a thousand. But, like most lures, the majority of these sell for less than $300.00.

Shakespeare made an early lure out of cork, then wood, then metal, called the Revolution. These trade for $300.00+. I also like the Evolution. It is a fish-shaped hard rubber lure made in the early years of Shakespeare into the 1930s. These sell for $300.00 – 500.00 most of the time (see front cover). Shakespeare really never produced a lot of spinning lures, instead, the company made its money on rods and reels during the spinning era. However, Shakespeare did offer us the Dopey and Grumpy from Snow White fame in spinning sizes in the early 1950s. In addition to these, look for: the Jack Smith lure, the Egyptian Wobbler, the naturalized finishes on its Torpedo and other lures, its unusual Pad-Ler Mouse, its common Shakespeare Mouse in a number of varieties, the Glo-Lite lures of plastic that glow in the dark, the early Pikie Kazoo lures, the interesting shaped (egg like) Waukazoo Wobbler, the Tantalizer, or any of the other unique Shakespeare offerings. Most lures by Shakespeare are unique and not like the other big six companies, and one will soon learn to recognize the quality of the older lures especially.

This company made a variety of spinners and related tackle and also entered the spinning lure fray with the manufacture of the Grumpy in ⅕ oz., 1¾" size. It was of course named after one of the seven dwarfs in the famed *Snow White* movie of the era. Shakespeare offered few baits specifically aimed at the spinning market as it started to concentrate more on its famous glass rods and Wondereels. However, the Grumpy is a nice early wooden spinning lure available in nice color patterns and a related lure, the Dopey, has sold recently for over $75.00 each, new in the box.

The lure that always comes to mind for Baby Boomers first is the Shakespeare Swimming Mouse, available in a number of sizes in both wood and the plastic Glo-Lite Mouse versions. The wooden sizes in 1952 included a ⅘ oz., 3¼" lure, a Junior at ⅝ oz., 2¾", and a Baby at ½ oz., 2½". The Glo-Lite Mouse was a ⅝ oz., 2¾" surface lure. The Glo-Lite Pup was a ½ oz., 2⅝" lure designed to dive deep. Other Shakespeare lures included: the Jerkin Lure (later just called the Jerk), a ⅗ oz., 4" surface bait; the Pop-Eye plunker type surface lure at ⅝ oz., 3½" length; the Shakespeare Special (Dalton Special) at both ½ oz. and ⅝ oz. and 3" and 4" lengths. One of my personal favorites is the Midget Spinner at ½ oz., 1⅞" long, designed to dive. The Dopey was a 4⁄10 oz., 1 5⁄16" lure that cast like a bullet and could even be used for spinning, designed to dive deep. The Pup was a ½ oz., 2⅝" deep diver as was the attractive Slim Jim at ⅗ oz., 3¾" long. The Slim Jim was a torpedo-shaped lure, and with its photo finish paint was beautiful. Saltwater offerings included the non-descript clothespin-type lure called the Wiggle Diver (made in plastic by Creek Chub later) and the attractive Sea Witch Midget. Shakespeare still produced all lures in wood in 1952 unless they were in the Glo-Lite series, which was plastic. Many of these lures are shown in *Modern Fishing Lure Collectibles, Volume 1*, and in this section.

Typical vintage Shakespeare boxes prior to 1950. $10.00 – 20.00 empty, depending on lure model.

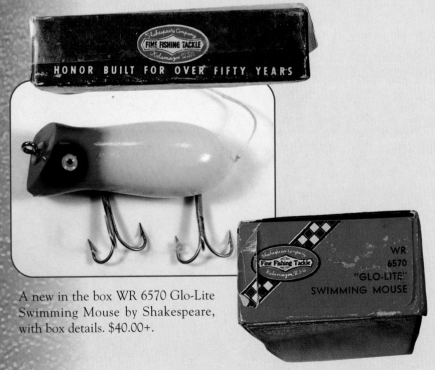

A new in the box WR 6570 Glo-Lite
Swimming Mouse by Shakespeare,
with box details. $40.00+.

104

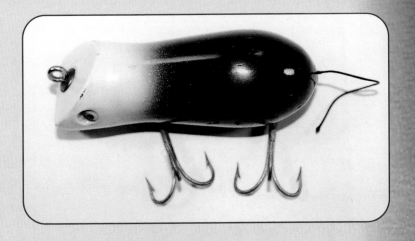

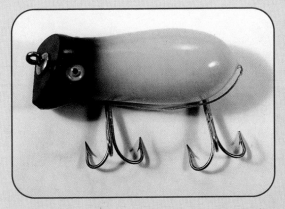

A Glo-Lite version in black head/white body, and a wooden version in white head/black body of the Swimming Mouse lure. $20.00 – 35.00 each.

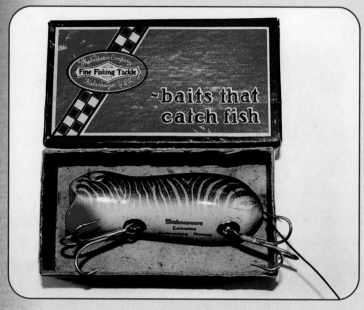

Nice tiger stripe pattern Shakespeare Swimming Mouse in wood, new in two-piece cardboard box. $60.00+.

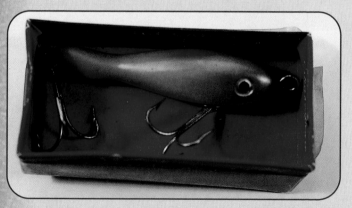

Very collectible Sea Witch Midget, Model 6534, in pretty Rainbow pattern, new in plastic top box from the 1950s. Sold online for over $80.00.

Model 6567 Jerkin Lure, SF (silver flitter), circa 1950. This also could be ordered as a 6567-S with spinner blade on tail. $20.00 – 40.00.

A nice Glo-Lite Pup lure in frog pattern, Model 6554 F (frog). Circa 1950, $25.00+.

Model 6602, Grumpy SF wood lure new in box. This is the 1¾", ⁴/₁₀ oz. lure described earlier. I have an entire color collection of these and they are outstanding lures. $30.00 – 50.00, new in box, some colors even more. They trade well loose also, selling for $20.00+ in most cases, if clean.

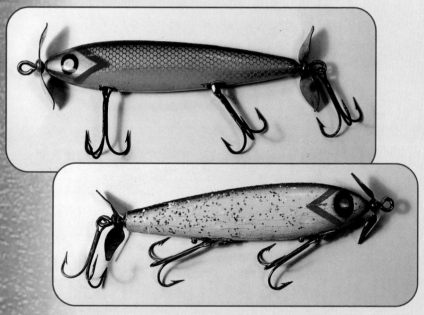

The Florida Shiner bait was produced by Shakespeare and a very similar model was made by Paw Paw. $20.00 – 40.00 according to 2004 sales.

The very attractive Model 6601, Midget Spinner wooden lure, circa 1950. $20.00 – 40.00.

One of the most attractive wooden lures from the 1970s is the Krazy Kritter, offered in both a sinking and floating model in seven standard colors. It was also available in a spinning model in a slightly different shape. Some lures are marked on belly as to brand and made in "Hong Kong," and others are not. Some are marked only "S" for sinking. $60.00 – 80.00 for excellent to mint ones, according to my own sales in 2003 – 2004.

Spinning Krazy Kritter, circa 1975, wooden lure. $40.00 – 60.00.

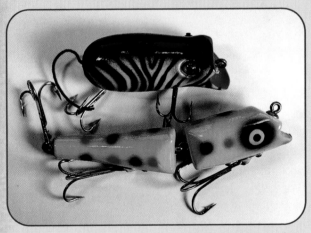

Note what happens when Shakespeare and Paw Paw get together, a Shakespeare Mouse with a new form in a Shakespeare color, and a Paw Paw Jointed Darter, now called a Shakespeare Dragon Fly, in traditional form with a new color! These lures are from 1975 and the last wooden lures made by Shakespeare. Actually quite rare, $30.00+ each.

Shakespeare's version of the Paw Paw Mister 13 from circa 1975. This is a plastic lure and very pretty. I sold a few for $25.00 – 40.00 depending on color, all mint to excellent.

Our final 1975 offering is a series of wooden Piky-Getum lures previously made by Paw Paw and put out as Shakespeare lures. These came in nine colors in 1975. I have sold them for $25.00 – 40.00 each, depending on color. Rainbow and Yellow with dots are stunning lures.

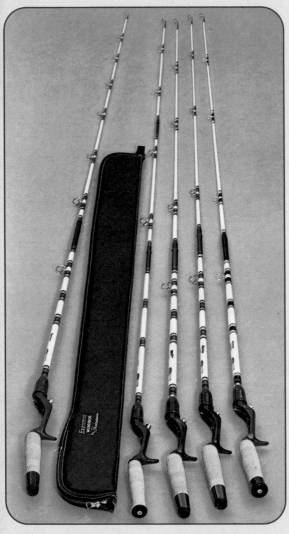

The reason Shakespeare concentrated on rods, the famous Wonderod in five models. Wonderods sell easily for $25.00 – 75.00.

A beautiful Slim Jim in the pretty photo finish pattern. Model 6541 was introduced in 1916 and still made in the early 1950s. One of the more collectible Shakespeare baits. $65.00 – 100.00 if boxed (this one has two-piece box).

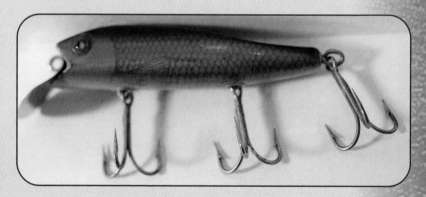

A Bass-A-Lure, also in a photo finish pattern. This earlier bait came with five baits I purchased, all from the first two decades of the 1900s. This was not produced after the war and is rare. $150.00 – 200.00.

113

An Evolution, the three-hook, fish-shaped lure in hard rubber from the first ⅓ of the last century. $300.00 – 600.00.

A unique set of baits for the Shakespeare collector to locate are these Marty's Silver Streak and Marty's Mouse lures from a car dealership in Wisconsin. Marty had them made by Shakespeare and he gave them away as gimmicks. The lures are common in northwest Wisconsin but not elsewhere. The Mouse is more common than the Darter. $40.00 – 60.00.

South Bend

South Bend is the last of the big six alphabetically and likely the third in terms of lure production and maybe even collectibility. This old Indiana company made a wide array of tackle, rods, reels, and lures. If it was to do with fishing, it could be purchased from South Bend at one time.

As many companies, it started with a couple of mainstay baits that built its reputation and pocket books. If one thinks of South Bend, one first thinks of a Bass-Oreno lure, or an early Vacuum bait. Millions of Bass-Oreno lures were made, and are still being made by Luhr Jensen & Sons. Other classic South Bend lures include: the Surf-Oreno, the Nip-I-Diddee, Pike-Orenos, Two-Orenos from 1937 onward, Tenite lures including the Better Bass-Orenos, the Fish-Obites (first lure with a written guarantee on the box side), Two-Obites in Tenite, my all time favorite, the Fin-Dingo, purchased from Ropher Tackle in 1951, the Fish-Oreno, the early 900 series minnows, and many more. South Bend also had an extensive fly rod lure line and many spinning lures.

There are fewer South Bend collectors than Heddon or Creek Chub collectors but the company is growing in popularity and it made beautiful lures. I do not think the varnish on them is as sound as on Creek Chub or Heddon lures but mint to excellent lures are all gorgeous. Of course the Tenite 2 lures are normally found in at least excellent minus condition, making them of interest to collectors as well. The Fin-Dingo is an example of a fairly short run lure for South Bend and that makes it more valuable. Many such short production run examples exist and one will learn that as the collection grows.

South Bend still exists today as a company but it only sells terminal tackle, rods, reels, and imported lures, mainly through discount and dollar store type chains. The famed Oreno line of baits was owned by Gladding, then Glen L. Evans, and is now owned by Luhr Jensen & Sons of Hood River, Oregon. Luhr Jensen is making a limited number of the lures in wood and plastic today.

Values for South Bend lures vary widely, if not wildly! Bass-Orenos are common, especially the easy colors such as red/white or the red/white arrow pattern. They trade for only $12.00 – 20.00 mint. However, many collectors underrate the early no-eye Bass-Orenos, actually worth two to three times this amount due to rarity. South Bend first made the lures without eyes, then glass eyes, then tack eyes, then carved eyes, then painted eyes, and then pupil changes become important. At the same time, hardware changed from cup to surface along the way.

115

Thus, eye and hardware variations become very important, as do color variations. Also, the early South Bend minnows are as pretty as any, and some of them are very rare, commanding hundreds of dollars each. Even the early no-name-on-propeller Surf-Orenos in Green Crackleback will command over $200.00 each in excellent condition. So, South Bend lures may be inexpensive on one hand, and fairly pricey on the other.

As to colors, there are many slight variations that are valuable. A particular orange stripe on the forward part of some of the Surf-Orenos is rare in one color pattern. A few of the blues are rare in Bass-Orenos, as is green. The Luminous lures are all hard to find in excellent to mint condition. Unlike Heddon, Green Crackleback is fairly scarce in South Bend's early lures. Of the 900 series minnows, the Hex pattern is likely the most rare. Red and yellow is rare on the Nip-I-Diddee, and blue and white is rare on most. Any of these colors will command a premium.

South Bend was one of the oldest and largest providers of fishing tackle in 1952. One thing I noted when doing an advertising review for another book is that South Bend had a minimum of ⅓ page of advertising in each issue examined from 1937 until 1952 (and likely beyond). Often South Bend used a full-page ad to introduce new items or simply give an array of its lures and reels and rods. South Bend also made a complete line of terminal tackle and it included all types of spinners in typical configurations, e.g. Colorado blades, Indiana blades, etc., most of which were marked. By 1952 South Bend had introduced the highly collectible Sunspot Spoon and also had the Trix Oreno line in ⅝, ⅞, and 2 oz. sizes. South Bend had not introduced a lot of spinning size lures yet, but one of note was the Wee-Nippee and also the Spin-I-Diddee, both smaller versions of the casting Nip-I-Diddee. The company also had the Lil' Rascal (named after a kid's comedic group) at ¼ oz., 2¾" long. All of these lures were made of wood with carved eyes by 1952. Packaging included the quonset-hut tubes as well as boxes.

In addition to the earlier baits mentioned above, South Bend continued its lure development and acquisition until selling out later to Gladding (the Line Company). It actually acquired my favorite lure and my lure-collecting nickname, Fin-Dingo, in 1951 – 1952. In addition to making some spinning lures, spoons, and spinners mentioned earlier, this company made a very complete line of baitcasting and trolling lures, including a few saltwater models. The list here may not be complete but it is the major line as still being made in 1952.

South Bend made a number of lures in Tenite for years, including the Fish-Obite, Two-Obite, and Bass-Obite. It also had one of the most complete lines of flies and fly rod baits. Its rod and reel line-ups were also complete and it sold all miscellaneous tackle as well. By 1952, the majority of lures were carved eye and surface hardware for the wooden models, and most were still made in wood. The Fin-Dingo was only made as a diving lure by South Bend and only in plastic. It was both a diver and floater in plastic when originally made by Ropher of Los Angeles. The Super Snooper was also a plastic lure by South Bend.

The most recognizable South Bend lure is likely the multi-million selling Bass-Oreno and its little offspring, the Babe-Oreno. A nice wooden surface lure is the Go Plunk, available in ⅜ oz. and 3" size. A much older surface lure by South Bend is its famous Surf-Oreno, and it was available in both a 1 oz., 3¾" size and the Midget Surf-Oreno at ¾ oz., 2¾". The famed Bass-Oreno was available in 1952 in standard ¾ oz., 3¾" length. The Babe-Oreno was ½ oz., 2¾" long. The Midge-Oreno was ⅜ oz., 2¼" long. The Zaragossa and Sarasota looking Be-Bop lure was available in two sizes at ½ oz. and ⅝ oz. and 3⅜" and 4½" lengths. The Pikie type Pike-Oreno was ⅝ oz. and 4¾" long. The Baby Pike-Oreno was ½ oz. and 3¾" long. The Jointed Baby Pike-Oreno was ½ oz., 4" long. The Big Jointed Pike-Oreno for Muskie fishing was 1½ oz., 6" long. The plastic Super Snooper was ½ oz. and 2⅞" long, shaped similar to a banana bait. The Dive-Oreno was available in three sizes with the same name, ½ oz., 3¼ oz. and 4 oz. versions. A unique lure that should gain in collectibility is the Explorer, a wooden crab that was ½ oz., 3¾" in its straight form and ½ oz. and 3⅞" in its jointed version. The Fin-Dingo came in six colors and was a plastic diving lure with fins and a single treble hook. It is well documented in *Modern Fishing Lure Collectibles, Volume 1*, but it was ½ oz. and 1½" long in the South Bend version. It was new to South Bend in 1951 – 1952.

The Fish-Obite lure was an early South Bend Tenite lure and came with a fish-catching guarantee. It was ⅖ oz. and 2⅜" long in 1952.

The two treble hook sizes did vary over the years and earlier models had two sizes available. The Fish-Oreno is an attractive deep diver with a metal head for weight and an extended line tie. It was ⅞ oz. and 3½" long, and came furnished with two #1/0 trebles in 1952. The Nip-I-Diddee was a nice surface lure and has gained popularity recently with collectors. It came with either three #4 doubles or with three trebles. By 1952, it was carved eye and came packaged in a quonset-hut similar to the Fin-Dingo packaging. It was ⅝ oz. and 3" long. South Bend lures are shown in *Modern Fishing Lure Collectibles, Volume 1*, in detail and in this section.

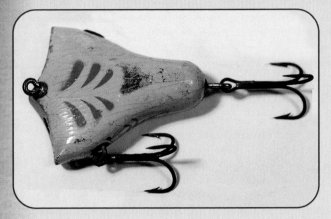

An early South Bend Vacuum bait. South Bend purchased many lures from other makers from this early Vacuum bait to the Fin-Dingo and Rock Hopper lures of more recent vintage. Even though not mint and a hook missing, these baits are rare and sell for $200.00 to over $1,000.00 with some regularity. To find one in the field would be a rare treat indeed.

Tough colored Bass-Oreno, luminous. Glass-eyed version post dates the no-eyed version. Many South Bend lures were marked as this one on the back. $50.00+, due to luminous paint.

King Bass-Oreno for salmon and other large game fishing, 4½"
long, carved eyes, through mouth heavy duty hardware, rear
hook swings free of hanger upon striking to prevent fish from
throwing the hook. $50.00+.

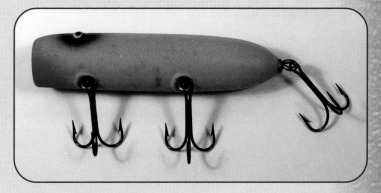

Orange Firelacquer Bass-Oreno. This is a rare color (and these
Gantron paint colors cannot be cleaned) in fine shape, tack eyes,
name on back, early 1950s. $100.00+ due to color.

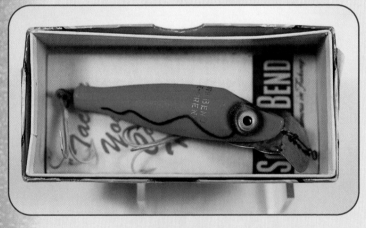

3¼" Dive-Oreno, carved eyes, surface hardware, in beautiful Firelacquer, Model No. G956 SNR, and rare introductory box. $150.00 plus due to introductory box and rare color and condition. Dive-Oreno lures trade for $30.00 – 50.00 in most colors.

Spin-I-Oreno in carved eye. This early 1950s small Bass-Oreno family lure is in a nice color. $15.00 – 20.00, more in original tube.

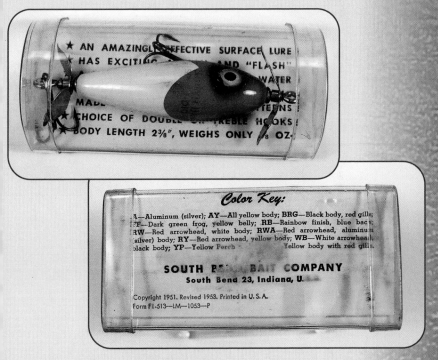

Model T-916 RW carved-eye Spin-I-Diddee in tube dated 1953. The T stands for treble hook version as these came with choice of treble or double hooks. Also, color RW is red arrowhead white body, not simply red and white. This quonset-hut type tube also housed the Spin-I-Oreno shown above and the Fin-Dingo lures and a few others in the early 1950s. $25.00 – 35.00 in tube.

Standard box type for 1930s – early 1950s lures. This box type was followed by a cardboard box with a plastic top, the tube shown on page 121, and a slide-top box. $10.00 – 20.00, as boxes are common.

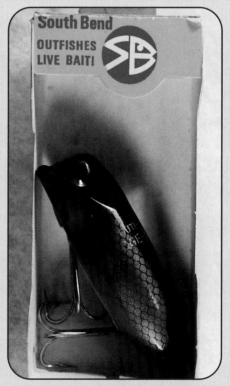

The Gladding style trademark, black dot, light blush around eyes, surface hardware, metal pin in tail, Midge-Oreno new in slide type box, Model 938 YP, 2⅜".
$20.00.

122

Nip-I-Diddee, carved eyes, double hooks. Early 1950s version of collectible wooden Nip-I-Diddee lure. $20.00 – 40.00 depending on color for the carved eyes. Remember, they came with both double and treble hooks.

Early wooden Plunk-Oreno in Rainbow with nice weighted fly attached (factory), 2⅛" long, highly desired lure. $100.00 – 150.00.

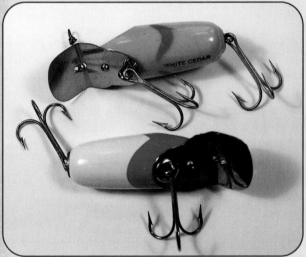

White Cedar Dive-Oreno. South Bend marked a few lures in the 1950s "White Cedar" as shown here (yellow one). These are the smallest size Dive-Orenos. $20.00 – 40.00 for most.

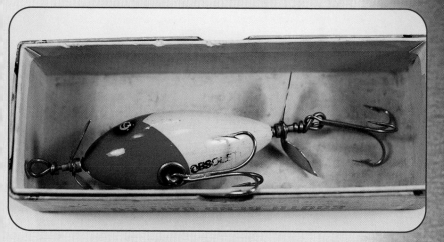

Obsolete Surf Oreno. South Bend marked a number of lures Obsolete when models changed or were discontinued. It makes a fun side-line in collecting. Baby Surf-Oreno in arrow pattern is common but the Obsolete is special. New in box, $75.00+.

Another thing South Bend did was to mark lures "Sub-Standard" for its seconds (Heddon marked them 2nd) on the box or even on the lure at times. Frankly, this Dive-Oreno in Yellow Perch, Model 954, is mint as far as I can tell. $50.00 – 75.00.

125

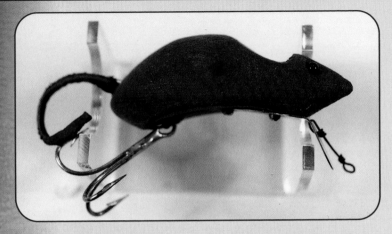

Tough to locate Mouse-Oreno by South Bend, 2¹¹⁄₁₆" long, bead eyes, leather tail, bottom of diving lip marked with South Bend, Mouse-Oreno, single treble, cup hardware, lip held on by two blade screws. $50.00+.

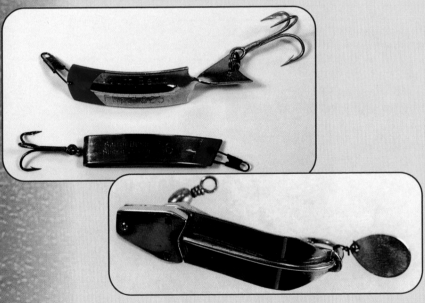

Not much value in these common South Bend metal lures (above and on page 127), a Flip-It, the Super-Duper, and the Trix-Oreno. Of these, the Trix-Oreno is in most demand. They made millions of them and they are very common. In the tube they will bring $10.00, loose only a buck or two each. The Trix-Oreno may bring more. I still use Super-Dupers for Brook Trout with great success, 14" opening day on one in 2000.

126

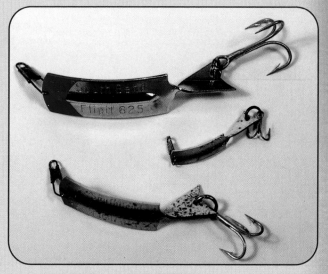

Flip-It.

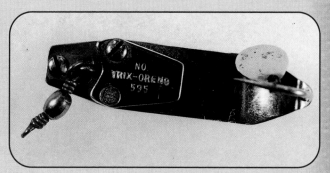

Trix-Oreno.

127

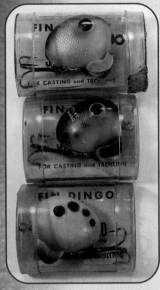

Three South Bend Model 1965s new in the tubes. Note the top tube is for a larger lure, but South Bend used it and then put a plastic tape label on the end to mark it as a Fin-Dingo. I would guess this is the first package type prior to casting a tube of a special size just for our little buddies. Colors are Green Perch (GP), Goldfish Scale (SG), and Yellow with black spots (YE). Six of the 12 Ropher colors that South Bend continued to make when purchasing the rights in 1951 – 1952. The lure was first advertised by South Bend in a May 1952 issue of *Field & Stream Magazine*. These are now competitive with plastic Punkinseeds selling for $50.00 – 100.00 most of the time, if mint.

Model 1991 WB, new from the box and box end. This Tenite lure was introduced in 1941 and came with a guarantee in writing. These have become very collectible. Early ones were Tenite 1 and will disintegrate, but most seem to be Tenite 2 and are fine. $30.00 – 65.00 with the Shad-O-Wave patterns bringing the most. The one shown would also bring about $65.00 as black and white lures are not common and it is mint in the box. I sold many loose ones in 2004 for $25.00 – 35.00.

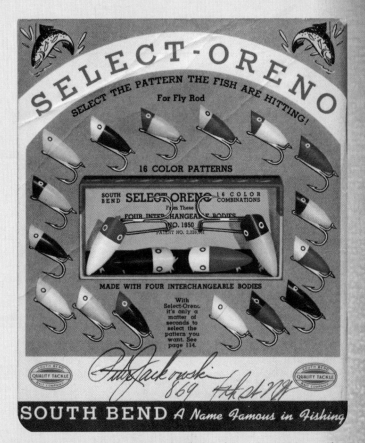

New in 1942, Select-Oreno South Bend Bait Company catalog, 1942 *Fishing – What Tackle and When*, back cover. Select-Oreno lures sell for $100.00+ if the four lure set is complete.

Four standard Optic colors, lures are 2¼" long, most are marked South Bend Optic and Pat Pend on bottom, with surface belly and simple screw hardware. These are examples of another collectible 1950s plastic bait from South Bend. $20.00+ each.

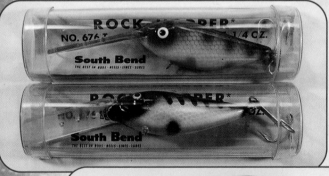

Two new Rock Hopper lures in tube and a loose one. The ones in the tubes are ¼ oz. models. The Model No. 676 T is a Trout and the Model No. 676 BB is a Blue Back. These lures were introduced in 1956 – 1957 and were actually developed by another company first. It is one of South Bend's last lures ever. $15.00 – 25.00 new in tube.

A very early South Bend Surf-Oreno in the nice Green Crackleback pattern, no name on propellers, heavy duty reinforced hardware, excellent condition, came from a group of very early lures. Sales of $200.00+ are common for this lure.

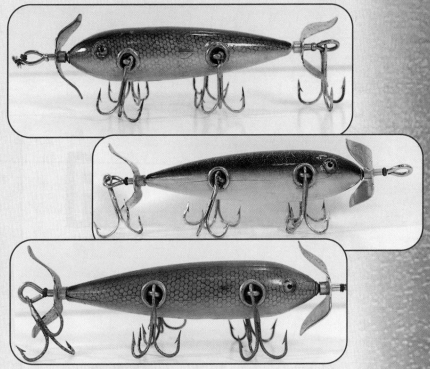

Three examples of the early 900 series underwater minnows. Even the one in rough shape is desirable as these lures are actually less common than their Heddon competitors. $200.00 – 600.00 covers most sales, Cracklebacks average about $400.00, and the Hex patterns and Sienna lures bring over $600.00. Of course the rougher one shown will not command this much and will sell for less than $100.00.

131

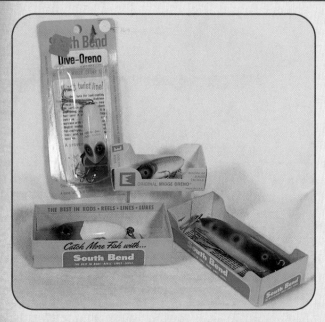

Four more recent packaging types used by South Bend and then Evans. Remember the Gladding box shown earlier. The carded Dive-Oreno is a wooden 1950s bait as is the Frog Bass-Oreno and the R/W (red arrow) Babe-Oreno. The Midge-Oreno is an Evans version after they bought out Gladding. Remember the lure rights went from South Bend to Gladding to Evans to Luhr Jensen where they now reside. All of these lures sold online in 2004 for $18.00 – 32.00 each, the Frog Bass-Oreno bringing the most.

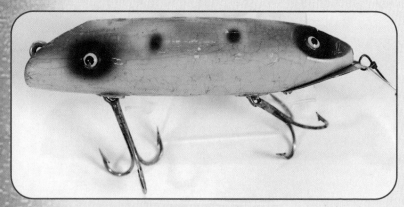

The Two-Oreno wooden lure was first produced in 1937. This frog spot is a little rough but a vintage South Bend lure in a nice color, tack eyes, cup rig. $18.00 – 30.00.

132

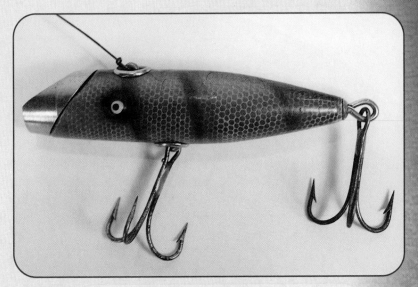

The Fish-Oreno with its heavy metal head/diving lip and line tie is in high demand by collectors. This one is tack-eyed in the Green Perch color and was in very good minus condition. Sold online in 2004 for $42.00. Range for these is about $40.00 – 100.00 for tack eye and double for glass eye models. Sales are recorded much higher for boxed lures.

A 1950s Spin-I-Diddee with carved eyes and double hooks. I like this color pattern and these lures do fairly well, but it is common. $12.00 – 20.00. This one sold for $18.00.

133

South Bend made two lines of fly rod baits, one in its name and one in its less expensive bait line called Best-O-Luck. I think these are both Best-O-Luck versions of the fly rod size Bass-Oreno. Fly rod wobblers such as this trade fairly well. $20.00+ each, up to $50.00 each if mint or excellent.

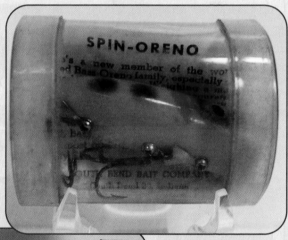

Two shots show another Spin-Oreno new in its quonset-hut in the pretty orange spot color. This early 1950s bait is wood with carved eyes and surface hardware. $25.00 – 35.00 in tube. Loose Spin-Orenos only sell for $12.00 – 15.00 as a rule.

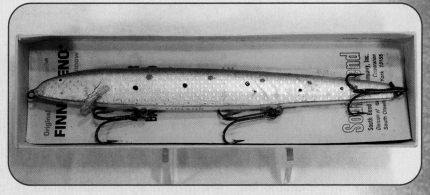

Our final example of a response to the Rapala from Finland. South Bend actually imported a balsa lure from Finland (bottom of lure marked as to country of origin) and called it, cleverly enough, the Finn-Oreno. These did not sell well as Rapala had the market cornered so they are actually quite scarce. This one has its celluloid type lip deteriorating, but is pretty nice overall. Sold online in 2004 for $28.00. I would rank these at $25.00 – 40.00 for mint lures in boxes.

Other Companies

The first part of this book has introduced the reader to the big six traditional lure companies. I would estimate that these comprise about 70% of all lures found in the field. That is an estimate, not a scientific fact. The location of an individual in the United States or elsewhere may change this. In other words, if in Missouri or Arkansas I would expect one to find more lures from Woods, Clark, or even Pico at times. But, the big six all aggressively advertised and marketed their lures nationally and internationally for 50 years or more. Thus, they are everywhere fishing is found.

This section shows fewer lures from as many companies as space allows. I have selected the companies based upon the idea of showing companies that the collector will likely find, not the super rare ones seldom seen by even more advanced collectors. I wish I could show you all of them but then this would not be a field guide, but a textbook or encyclopedia of lures instead.

I have listed the remaining companies alphabetically and believe that they are the most important ones in general lure collecting. The choice was mine and is based upon buying and selling thousands of lures and looking for lures in the field for over ten years. I know what is out there, I know what one tends to see at auctions and in garage sales, I know what is hot and what is not. All of these variables went into my decision to include a company in this section. Clearly, I could have added many more if space would have allowed, but it does not in a brief guide such as this.

Also, as with the big six, I have used 1952 as a benchmark based upon extensive research done for another book, and have gone back in history from there, and forward, depending on the company. The nice thing about the year 1952 is that it is absolutely transitional from bait-casting to spinning and often times from wooden lures to plastic ones for some companies. Of course, many 1952 companies only produced plastic lures, as the technology developed so rapidly right after the war years.

So, if your favorite company is not in this section, blame me. But, if you already have a favorite company you likely know something about it and have a catalog or some means to identify the lures. This section will help you identify at least 80% of all the remaining lures if we measure by volume as found in the field.

Allcock

An early Allcock spinner is on the left side of the front cover. It is one of a few collectible metal baits. The one shown was made by Allcock and is valued at about $200.00. However, metal baits are not in great favor with most collectors. I am not going to cover metal baits in this book for this reason and because they are so diverse. But, as a general rule some metal baits are highly valued such as this one and others by Allcock. Additional important companies include: Abbey & Imbrie, Biff, Buel (inventor of spoon in 1800s), Chapman, Comstock, Haskell, Lowe, Pflueger, Shakespeare, and Winchester. There are many more but this is a start.

Metal baits trade for the most part for $5.00 – 10.00, but early metal baits of quality will quickly reach into the hundreds of dollars. One must study them to be able to differentiate them, and a good metals book such as that by Carter is recommended. Modern metal baits seldom sell for more than $5.00 without a box and $20.00 with a box.

Al Foss (American Fork & Hoe)

True Temper Corp. of Geneva, Ohio, owned the rights to this line of lures and rods by 1952. Al Foss offerings were primarily weighted casting lures with spinner propellers. In 1952 the main offerings were the Dixie Wiggler, the Oriental Wiggler, and the Shimmy Wiggler. The Dixie Wiggler was a crawfish type body with a Foss type propeller and a single dressed hook with a double week guard. The Oriental Wiggler was the famed celluloid pork rind bait made by Foss in a variety of colors, pure white, pure red, red/white, and black/white, to name a few. It had two glass eyes, a Foss propeller, and a single hook with a double weed guard and a pork rind attachment. The Shimmy Wiggler was more of a mouse-shaped spoon bait with a Foss propeller and a single dressed with a double weed guard (similar to an Evan's Herb's Dilley Bait). True Temper also offered the Speed Shad in a Speed Shad, Jr. version for spinning at ¼ oz., 1⅞" length.

As stated earlier, not a lot of interest exists for metal baits, but some of the earlier Al Foss baits are in demand and more people likely collect these metal and celluloid baits than most metal baits. Some of the lures are actually quite rare and the tin boxes are always hard to find in excellent or better condition. Most of the early metal offerings were gone by 1952.

In 1948 two nice baitcasting lures were added to the line that are very collectible. The Crippled Shad was a surface lure meant to represent an injured minnow, weighing ½ oz. at 2¾" long. They were packaged at the time in an attractive two-piece cardboard box. The Speed Shad was designed to dive deep and was ½ oz. and 2⅜" long. It is collectible in its original offering and also as made later by Bomber Bait Co.; now Pradco owns the rights to these lures.

In the corners are three of the five Al Foss tin box colors: red, blue, and green (white and orange are not shown). Across the top are a: Bass Pop, all white Oriental Wiggler, a No. 9 Jazz Wiggler/canvas skirt, two more Orientals and a No. 9 Jazz Wiggler Jr. In the next row: three styles of the Little Egypt (oldest left to right) and another Bass Pop. Around the box papers are six No. 11 and No. 12 Frog Wigglers, including one all brass one. On the left border are several sizes of Shimmy Gals and on the right a Ponca blade New Egypt, a black and white Oriental, and a Little Minnie. Near the bottom are a Fan Dancer, some Dixie Wigglers, a Sheik, and a rare No. 6 Shimmy. Al Foss baits should bring more than they do considering their age, but they suffer from the dreaded "metal bait syndrome" of collectors holding prices down. Most of the baits commonly trade for only $20.00 or so, often times less. Some of the rare versions will command over $50.00 if wanted by a collector in the know.

Arbogast

Fred Arbogast & Co. was located at 313 W. North St., Akron, Ohio, still in 1952, and its main spinning lure offerings included the No. 1 and No. 2 Hawaiian Wigglers in ¼ oz., Hula Popper in ¼ oz., and the famed Jitterbug in ⅜ oz. size. In addition, the Hawaiian Wigglers were available in No. 1, No. 2, and No. 3 in casting weights. Additional bait casting lures still on the market included: the Hula Popper, available in ⅝ oz., 2¼" length for baitcasting, the Jitterbug, available in a ⅝ oz., 3" size for casting, and a 1¼ oz., 5" size for Musky fishing. The 1952 version of the Musky size had 3 #2/0 hooks.

Only the Musky size was made of wood in 1952. Hula Poppers were always made in plastic and Jitterbugs were primarily made in plastic. The Hula Dancer was a sinking lure weighing ⅝ oz., 2" long. The Hula Diver was another deep sinking lure weighing ⅝ oz., 3¼" long.

I detailed Arbogast lures and the company history in my *Volume 1*. To a Baby Boomer, this company made two lures most likely to be remembered: the Jitterbug and the Hula Popper. Any young boy or girl fishing for bass in the 1950s knew how to use these two lures, and usually with success! Jitterbugs make a fascinating collection due to color variations, lip variations, and material variations related to the war years. Also, they were made in both wood and plastic. Hula Poppers, on the other hand,, were only commercially made in plastic and do not have as much variation, but some certainly exists as to name location on the lure.

Earlier offerings of the Tin Liz series of baits are very collectible, and some very expensive. The little Tin Liz lures that look like a Walleye, a Pike, a Sunfish, and a Bluegill all bring over $200.00 each, usually approaching $300.00 or more per lure. I paid $300.00 recently for a Pike that is only excellent on one side; they are rare, it is that simple. Even fly rod Tin Liz lures sell for over $20.00 and the ones with glass eyes sell for $50.00 or more.

Of all of the companies in this section, Arbogast is likely the one most often found. The company distributed and advertised nationally. It advertised aggressively and even used special address codes in its ads to see which magazine people were ordering from, e.g. which ad paid off for them. I have found no less than a dozen examples of this advertising ploy.

One point of caution is that Jitterbugs and Hula Poppers are still being made by Pradco (they now own the company) so beware of recent offerings. Also, lures from the 1950s – 1970s though collectible, need to be in pristine condition to hold their higher values. Many rare colors exist from this time but one must make sure of condition. Finally, look for the Wheedler (later Wampum) lure and the Hula-Hoople lure, two lures from the 1960s that are very rare.

It is difficult to even begin to show all of the important variations of Arbogast lures in a field guide, but a few photos will help identify items. At least most of the baits are marked, making it easier for the collector. However, the frog colored Hula-Hoople is not marked, nor are some others.

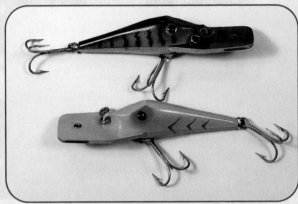

Arbogast Hustler lures. $12.00 – 20.00 each.

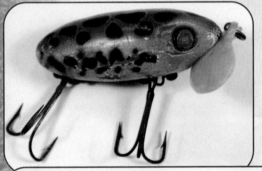

Rough shape but yellow plastic lip wooden Jitterbug in correct box from the war era, thin hardware type. $40.00 as is, but $100.00+ if excellent or better. Wooden Jitterbugs are scarce, war era wooden ones with plastic lips even moreso. Box alone is worth at least $20.00.

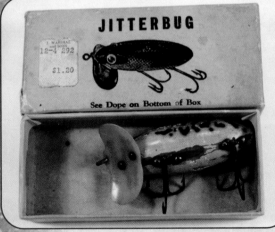

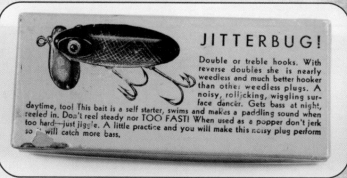

JITTERBUG!

Double or treble hooks. With reverse doubles she is nearly weedless and much better hooker than other weedless plugs. A noisy, rollicking, wiggling surface dancer. Gets bass at night, daytime, too! This bait is a self starter, swims and makes a paddling sound when reeled in. Don't reel steady nor TOO FAST! When used as a popper don't jerk too hard—just jiggle. A little practice and you will make this noisy plug perform so it will catch more bass.

Very rare color Fireplug Jitterbug, new in the box with hang tag, from the early 1950s, a yellow shore from the same time period, and a box bottom from the Fireplug. Fireplug, $75.00 – 125.00; Yellow Shore, $40.00 – 50.00, mint in box. Common color, so only about $15.00 loose.

A neat colorful display of spinning size, ¼ oz., Model 770 Spinning Hula Poppers showing typical Arbogast color patterns. $8.00 – 15.00 each.

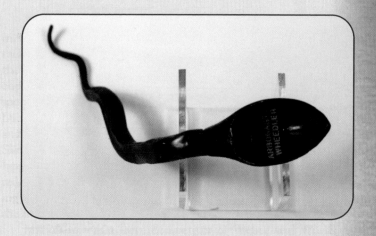

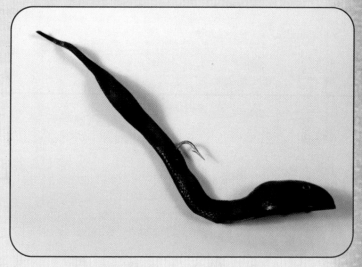

Very rare Wheedler lure. $75.00+.

143

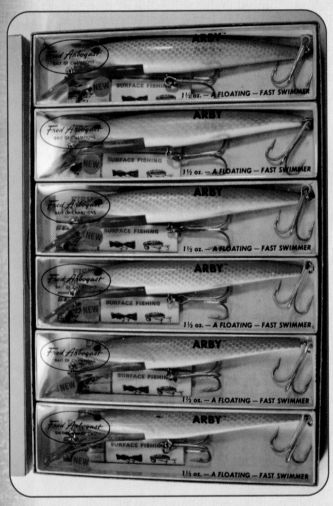

A six-pack of new in the introductory box Arbys from 1971. $15.00 – 20.00 each lure, $120.00 – 150.00 for six pack in mint shape such as this.

Bomber Bait Co.

The Bomber Bait Co. started in the war era and this company of Gainesville, Texas, made the famed Bomber still being used to catch bass and other game fish today (now owned by Pradco). Bomber made three baits in 1952 suitable for spinning, the Baby Bomber at ¼ oz., 2 ½", the Midget Bomber at ¼ oz., 2¾", and the Midget Bomberette at ¼ oz., 1¾". In 1952 they were all wooden lures.

Bomber also made a wide array of casting lures and they have all gained collectible interest in recent years. The color variations are nearly endless and some of the lures are difficult to find in any condition, let alone mint. The Bomber surface lures are some of the toughest to find and include the Knothead plunker type lure in both ⅜ oz. and ½ oz. sizes at 2¼" and 3¼" respectively. The Top Bomber was available in ⅜ oz. and ½ oz. sizes at 2⅜" and 3¼" lengths. The floating/diving Bomber was available in ⅜ oz. and ½ oz. sizes at 3¼" and 4¼". The Bomberette was available in ⅜ oz. and ½ oz. in 2¾" and 3¼" sizes. A ⅝ oz., 4¼" Bomber was also available in 1952. The Bombers were all originally wooden with no eyes. In 1949 they experimented with plastic and the plastic diving lipped "49ers," as collectors call them, are very valuable, as not many were made and they did not work well for fishing. In 1952 all of the models were again made in wood and had painted eyes. The models did not really change much until being made in plastic in the early 1970s. Pradco still produces the baits in mass numbers.

See my *Volume 2* for photos and a fine history of the company written by my friend and co-author of another book, John A. Kolbeck. As with other 1950s baits, collectors get pretty picky about condition with Bombers. One little chip on a diving lip caused by the Luxon line tie hitting it will decrease value.

But there are some really rare colors and the 49er plastic lip ones sell for $50.00 – 100.00 easily, so lures need not be from 1920 to be valued. I sold many Bombers in early 2004 after finding a selection of Dealer Dozens and they were all new in the box lures from 1965 – 1970 and some sold for as much as $50.00 each (the purple sparkles being a great color). I also sold a no-eye early box example for $68.00 empty in early 2004. I would say my average loose Bomber lures sell for $8.00, with some bringing a bit over $20.00. However, beat up Bomber lures bring only a buck or two as they certainly are not rare.

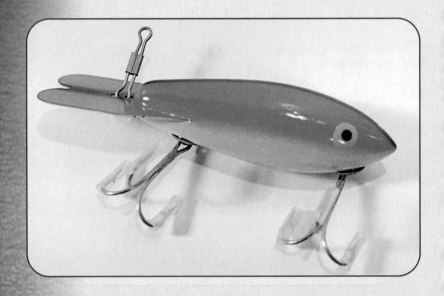

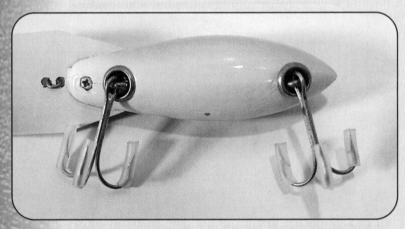

A nice rainbow colored Bomber given to me by my friend John since I collect Rainbow Lures of all types. Note the screw-in bottom of the lure in the second photo; this is the easy way to know if a Bomber or Waterdog is wooden with one quick glance. $20.00 – 30.00 as Rainbow is always a good color. Most colors average closer to $12.00 – 15.00 per loose lure.

Bomber Spinstick commemorative lure put out by Bass Pro Shops for their 30th anniversary in two-piece cardboard box. These are already trading for $25.00 – 35.00 each, new in box. It shows the typical white coach dog pattern and painted eye nicely. $25.00 – 35.00.

Wooden Bomber in yellow coach dog, new in older plastic slide-top box with papers. $15.00 – 20.00 as color is common.

Nice color in a Bomber lure is the Rainbow Trout as in this Pinfish lure, a plastic bait. I have sold a few Bombers in Rainbow Trout for $30.00+, and I would expect this one to do well. $25.00 – 35.00, more if boxed.

147

Paul Bunyan Bait Co.

The Paul Bunyan Bait Co., 1307 Glenwood Ave., Minneapolis, Minnesota, made the classic 66 Lucky Lure for casting. In 1952 they also made it in a spinning, or "midget" size at ¼ oz., a Baby Shiner lure in ⅛ oz., and the Minnie lure in ⅛ oz. Spoons included the Flash-Eye in treble, single, and weedless hooks; the Ruby Spoon in treble or single hooks; the Ole Olson in weedless single only; and the giant- sized Tear Drop in treble or single hooks.

In addition to the above metal and spinning lures, Paul Bunyan made an extensive array of fly rod, spinning, and baitcasting lures. It also made sinkers and reels (or at least packaged and marketed them). Its red box with Paul Bunyan on it is very attractive and collectible.

The company was covered in detail in my *Volume 1*. Lures included the River Runt type Weaver floating surface bait at ⅝ oz., 3⅜". The Weaver is a very attractive floating lure with ridges across the back of the body, making it unique in the runt type. It also came in a deep diving model called the Deep Weaver at ⅝ oz., 2⁹⁄₁₆" long. The Transparent Dodger was a slender diving bait with a slightly concave belly. The Ladybug is very collectible, usually bringing at least $25.00 for a good one and it came in diving and weedless versions as well. One of the most difficult baits to find in good shape is the Paul Bunyan Minnow made out of fragile celluloid. I actually had one of these break into dozens of pieces recently after being jostled around in a move. The rest of the Paul Bunyan baitcasting baits are made of durable plastic, but the Minnow is celluloid. Some of the fly rod baits are wood, many are plastic.

Paul Bunyan baits are very collectible and the Ladybugs and most of the plastic lures are trading for $20.00 – 30.00 each, at least. One nice thing about the Ladybugs is that they were preceded by both the Bates and even earlier the Lauby company wooden offerings. Bates converted them to plastic and all of the Bunyan Ladybugs were plastic. But the early Lauby types were wood and quite rare. This gives one a lure type that represents three companies and makes for an interesting collecting diversion.

The grandfathers of Paul Bunyan lures were Lauby Lures as shown here. These wooden lures were first made then the company was sold to Bates then to Paul Bunyan. Bates started making them in plastic and Paul Bunyan continued plastic production for all but the Dyna-Mite lure and one Popper which was recently discovered in wood. Lauby lures sell for $100.00 – 300.00 and are rare.

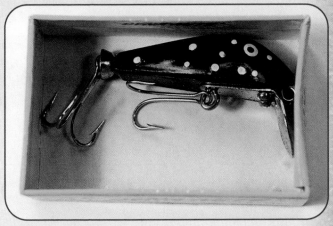

One of Paul Bunyan's few wooden lures, a Dyna-Mite in blue with white spots. $20.00 – 30.00.

149

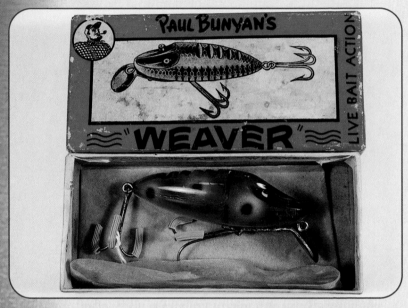

Translucent frog spot Weaver in colorful box. Weaver lures were stamped Paul Bunyan on the bottom. $25.00 – 40.00 in box.

Large and small Lady Bugs in orange with black spots. These evolved from the Lauby wooden spoons shown on page 149. $25.00 – 35.00 each.

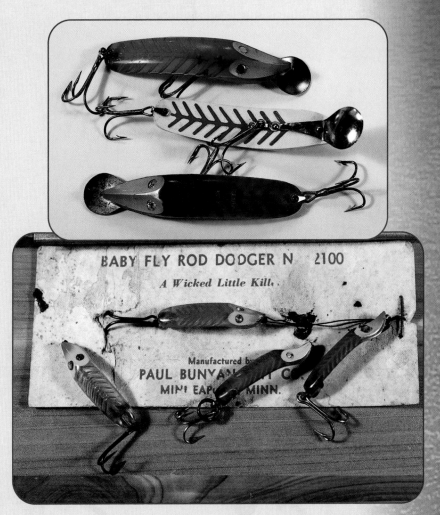

Large artful and transparent Dodgers and fly rod Transparent Dodgers, one new on card in neat Don Gapen fly box from the early 1950s, made in Michigan. Note especially the beauty of the translucent colors. The large Dodgers are valued at $10.00 – 20.00, and the fly rod models trade for a range double that amount.

Durable Plastics, Inc.
(Whopper Stopper Lures)

Durable Plastics, Inc., Box 793, Sherman, Texas (Whopper Stopper Lures) offered a spinning version of its Whopper Stopper at ¼ oz. in 1952. I documented this company in some detail in Volume 1. The surface popper, known as a Whopper-Stopper Topper (#200), was ⅜ oz., 2¼" with two trebles. The Whopper-Stopper #500 was ⅝ oz., 3⅝" long, the #100 was ½ oz., 3⅝", and the #400 was ⅝ oz., 4". The Baby Minnow, #500M, was ⅜ oz., 2¼" long. All Whopper-Stopper lures were only made in plastic and became some of the most successful of all bass baits through the years. Additional lures were developed after 1952 including the early bass spinner, the Dirty Bird, or its cousin, the Whirly Bird spinner. Also, a colorful bait to compete with the Rapala was developed in 1962 called the Hellcat.

Whopper Stopper made a number of special colors that bring two to three times the normal lure price, e.g. Hellbenders new in boxes from 1955 often sell for $20.00 or more and a special color would sell for $40.00 – 60.00 easily. This is true of most special color lures in other companies as well, of course. Whopper Stopper even made a neat little red plastic tackle box marked with its name. These are quite uncommon.

The two most common, and also most collected, of the Whopper Stopper lures are the Hellbender and the Bayou Boogie. I sell a lot of these lures new in the pre-zip code boxes for $20.00 – 40.00 each. Post-zip code versions drop some in price but the special colors are in high demand. Whopper Stopper did not invent the Bayou Boogie but it bought the rights to the lure fairly early in the 1950s from the A. D. Mfg. Company of St. Louis, Missouri. The earlier lure came in a nice orange/white two-piece cardboard box with a picture of a cartoon type fish on the top.

Another collectible bait from this company is the Hellraiser lure, a top water lure in the same color patterns, for the most part, as the Hellbenders. These lures trade a little stronger than the Hellbenders and Bayou Boogies as they were made for a shorter time period.

This purple sparkle color sells well in Hellbenders and is shown with a modern patch for the Governor's Open in Wisconsin in 1998 (Hon. T. Thompson, now Secretary of Health and Human Services) which was held behind my farm where I normally fished opening day. Patch, $10.00. Hellbender in purple, $25.00 – 40.00, new in the box. I have sold dozens of new in box Hellbenders from a closed tackle shop, and they bring $15.00 – 40.00 for most colors.

A collectible Whirlybird Spinner Model 1209. This lure was one of my surprises, selling online in 2003. I received over $30.00 each for many of these early bass baits and then found out one person was buying them to fish. According to him they suspend off the bottom better than any known bass bait, and he was tickled to find some. However, collectors were also bidding on them and a couple went for over $40.00 each. At that point I decided to keep one of each color I had. $25.00 – 40.00 new in box.

A 6007 Bayou Boogie and a small Hellbender Model 1012. These are two examples from about 15 dealer dozens I purchased from a closed store. The Bayou Boogies sold for $18.00 – 36.00 each, and the Hellbenders for $12.00 – 24.00 unless an "S" color, then for over $40.00.

Horrocks-Ibbotson (Abbey & Imbrie)

Horrocks-Ibbotson, Utica, New York, advertised itself as the largest tackle company in the world and indeed made all types of terminal tackle, rods, reels, lines, miscellaneous items, and a complete line of lures. The company made many fine spinning lures, spinners, and spoons, including a Spinning Devon in spinning and casting sizes. Look for H-I spinners on their cards as they are still found in many tackle boxes. Spoons by H-I included the Drone, the Baspoon, Pearl Wobblers, and the Del Rey Wobbler. The Drone and the Baspoon were both available in spinning sizes, besides the traditional casting and trolling models.

In addition, H-I continued the earlier Abbey & Imbrie offerings of Go-Getter lures in casting sizes made of wood until not making lures any longer in 1960. H-I also made a very collectible wooden lure in the late 1920s called a Shmoo, named after the Lil' Abner cartoon character. The wooden lure offerings were limited in colors (four standard colors were offered) but wide in style and shape. H-I continued A&I packaging and the trade name after buying out the company in 1930, so it is difficult to tell an A&I lure from an H-I lure if in a Go-Getter box.

Also, of course, A&I sold lures made by Heddon, Creek Chub, and others. A&I never made its own lures but they are very desirable as collector pieces due to the relative rarity of them. H-I did indeed make its own lures according to my research but it also purchased lures for resale from Arnold Baits of Paw Paw, Michigan, and others as well.

The Go-Getter lures trade for $60.00 – 80.00 each in the attractive window box shown here. Loose they tend to sell for very little, as most people cannot identify them with any certainty. They are often thought to be Paw Paw lures, which they are not. Part of the confusion lies in the fact that Paw Paw bought Arnold and produced nearly identical lures after that point. The only sure way to know a Go-Getter is to find one in the field in the correct box. However, the color patterns are fairly unique to H-I and assist the collector as do the lure sizes once known. My new *Volume 3* will have a complete chapter on H-I and catalog reprints of its lures from 1949.

A&I or H-I Go-Getter wobbler in one of the few standard colors. I have noted the lures with the red blush over the eye are a bit earlier but H-I bought A&I in 1930 so this could be either company's lure. $60.00 – 80.00 boxed. Loose lures tend to sell for only $12.00 – 20.00, as folks do not know the maker. These lures are never marked in any way.

H-I wooden wobbler lure in Red Head/Yellow Scale, one of the H-I standard colors of the 1940s – 1950s. About the same size as a Babe-Oreno but cut a little differently. Note how far back the belly hardware is on some H-I lures. $20.00+ in this shape, more if identified properly.

156

Another new in box Go-Getter in one of the standard green scale colors of both A&I and H-I. The two most common H-I colors are this one and red/white. Even though the colors were few, the lure shapes were many, with nearly every shape of Heddon, Creek Chub, and Paw Paw type baits represented. $60.00 – 80.00 boxed.

A 1950s H-I wobbler type. Note the simplified hardware now on this one. $12.00 – 20.00.

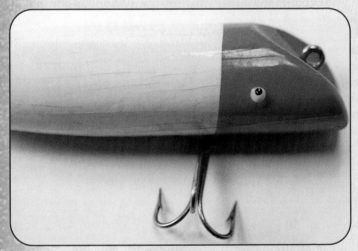

A close-up of the larger two-treble hook version of the Bass-Oreno type H-I lure, showing its eye and how the mouth is cut. $12.00 – 20.00.

Helin Tackle Company

The Helin Tackle Company of Detroit, Michigan, changed the fishing world with its Flatfish lure. When Charles Helin invented the Flatfish and gave a few to local fishing guides in 1937 – 1938 to try them out, his future was sealed. A simple wooden banana-shaped lure with multi-gang hooks became one of the all-time bestselling lures in the world. A Michigan tackle box cannot be found without a Flatfish or a Dardevle! He went from selling a few to a few million, literally within two years.

Over the years, dozens of offerings were available with complex offerings on the market in terms of models, colors, and hook gangs. Later Helin would invent the Swimmerspoon and the Fishcake. Both of these lures are very collectible. Ten years ago no one wanted to collect Flatfish, similar to Bombers five years ago, however, now there are a number of folks attempting to put together the extensive color collection it would take to have them all. I have sold Flatfish new in the box (pre-Zip boxes) for up to $35.00 each. Most sell for $6.00 – 12.00, however, the $9.00 – 18.00 range is fairly common for better colors or odd models. The natural frog is a beautiful color and fairly rare in Flatfish (sold one for $35.00+). Also, the Gantron color versions are more valuable as on all lures. The boxes vary greatly but the 1952 box was made for only one year and was a white box with a plastic top. See my *Volume 2* for a complete box history. Some of the early pre-patent boxes sell for $10.00+ empty.

Swimmerspoon and Fishcake lures sell for $8.00 – 30.00. A Fishcake new in the box may bring close to $50.00 if a more difficult color. A color collection of either one is a nice addition to a modern lure collection.

Flatfish are still being made and were made in the millions, so know what you are buying before spending too much. However, the collectibility of this common lure is well established now, and I would not scoff at picking up a few new in the box models at least. I would not pay more than $2.00 – 6.00 each for most post-zip code models, but some of the pre-zip models easily are worth $12.00 – 20.00 each. Even some rare colors in post-zip models will command higher prices.

Yellow Fish Cake, Model #9, 2¼". $25.00 – 40.00.

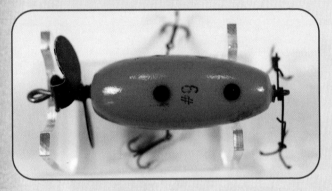

Orange Fish Cake, Model #9, 2¼", typical Helin gang hooks with simple screw hardware, front propeller. $25.00 – 40.00.

A nice Fishcake in the introductory box for a spinning size. $40.00 – 60.00 as frog is desired and introductory box increases value too.

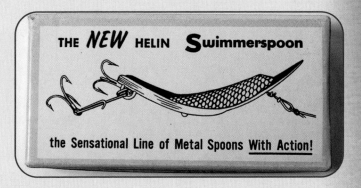

THE **NEW** HELIN **Swimmerspoon**

the Sensational Line of Metal Spoons With Action!

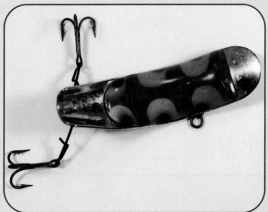

Introductory box for the Swimmerspoon, one new in same box, Model SP 175 SS, 1¾" long, and two more. The larger one is 2¼" long, Model 225. $18.00 – 25.00 boxed. I did sell one fly rod size in strawberry spot for over $25.00 without a box.

A variety of Flatfish boxes and a Model F5 FR (frog) Flatfish new (hook removed for shipping by Helin). I have a gross of these with no hooks; hooks were included to be added after shipping depending on size wanted, but I do not think this was a common practice. Sold in a pre-zip cardboard box with plastic top. See text for values; most are valued at only $4.00 – 8.00 boxed. However, the older two-piece boxes with lures are selling for $12.00 – 40.00 each, and I have sold some wooden Flatfish without boxes for nearly $20.00 if excellent.

162

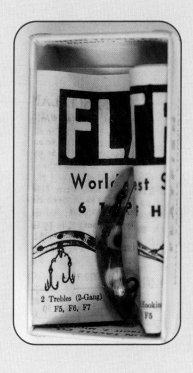

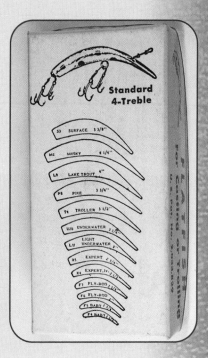

Kautzky Mfg. Co., Inc. (Lazy Ike)

Kautzky Mfg. Co., Inc., 522 Central Ave., Fort Dodge, Iowa made its lure, The Lazy Ike, available in ¼ oz., 2½" length and ⅛ oz., 2" versions by 1952. They were still made of wood at this time. Lazy Daze was originally called a Lazy Ike too made by a different company in Minnesota (switched names and became plastic). Kautzky later added many spinning sizes and made lures in plastic too, and developed the famed Natural Ikes in plastic. Packaging was originally in a two-piece cardboard box and later was in a cardboard box with a plastic top.

For baitcasting, the Lazy Ike was also still made only in wood in 1952 and was available in a ½ oz., 3" size and the Husky Ike was ⅝ oz., 3½" long. These lures are similar to Flatfish in their commonality but not quite as common. Collector interest has really picked up for new in the box wooden examples and even loose ones are selling for $6.00 – 10.00 regularly. I sold a number of Lazy Ike lures for $8.00 – 20.00 in boxes and loose in 2004.

In addition to the traditional offerings, this company offered the very collectible Sail Shark lure as its own after buying the rights from the Demon Lure Company of Texas. Then it developed the natural fish appearing Natural Ikes as its last major offering before being purchased by Pradco. The Sail Sharks sell for $15.00 – 30.00 loose and the Natural Ikes for $12.00 – 20.00 loose. Boxed lures naturally bring more.

Though of more recent vintage, the lures are now collectible and certainly should be in this guide, as one will find these lures very often in the field, at auctions, and in tackle boxes.

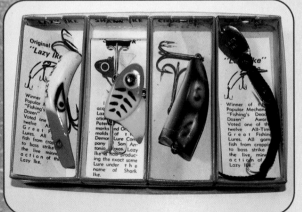

A more valuable Lazy Ike item, a "Bass Kit," with a Lazy Ike plastic worm, a Series 200 Shark Ike, a Chug Ike, and a Lazy Ike-2. $40.00 – 60.00.

A more uncommon plastic Lazy Ike lure, the Skitter Ike, with protruding eyes, simple screw hardware, 3" long, and marked on bottom. $8.00 – 12.00.

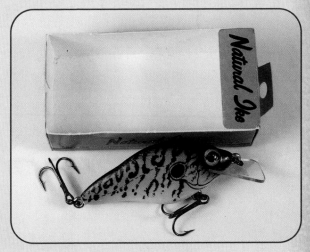

A collectible Natural Ike, these were a short run for the company and were made in many sizes and natural fish finishes. Early in 2001 I sold a collection of 22 of them for $14.00 each, and one usually gets more when just selling one or two lures at a time. This one is a Model NIM 25 MA (Medium Diver), new in slide-top plastic cardboard blue box that was standard for the Natural Ikes. See the 1980 BassPro Shops catalog for a complete color display of these colorful lures. Tike Ike lures (ultra light) are selling for over $40.00 each, and I now sell loose Natural Ike lures for $12.00 – 20.00 each. I would value any boxed Natural Ike from $25.00 – 35.00.

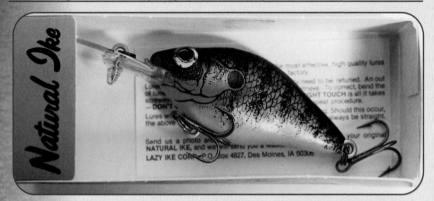

Another Natural Ike lure new in the box, the pretty sunfish color. $25.00 – 35.00.

An ultra light Shark Ike, Model 140, new in the introductory box after purchasing the rights from Demon Lures of Texas. $30.00 – 45.00 due to early box.

A more common 200 Shad new on a Lazy Ike card, $25.00 – 35.00 due to early card.

A Lazy Ike Sail Shark selling online in March 2004 for $16.00 in only very good minus condition due to rusty hooks and one pointer.

L & S Lures

Harold LeMaster first lived in and operated out of Kankakee, Illinois, and did not develop a box or sell lures commercially until 1937. Shortly thereafter, he took on a partner by the name of Phil Schriner and the two of them continued to make similar wooden, glass-eyed minnows from LeMaster's basement until 1941. The LeMaster Jointed Shiner was being made in 3" and 4½" sizes and in just four colors: red/white; yellow; green; and brown in 1941. Like many small companies (and large ones too), the company did not produce any lures during the war era.

LeMaster and Schriner officially formed the L & S Bait Company in 1946 and a new tradition was born as the lures were now produced only in plastic. From 1937 until 1946 all of the lures had been made in LeMaster's basement in Kankakee. However, growing demands forced the new company to open a factory in Bradley, Illinois, to produce its new line of plastic L & S lures.

During this period the company produced its now famous series of lures known as the Pike-Master and Bass-Master. These were first introduced as sinking models, then in floating models. According to an advertisement in the February 1949 issue of *Field & Stream*, L & S offered the Bass-Master, Pike-Master, Muskie-Master, and a saltwater Trout-Master for $1.40 each by 1949. Then came the Panfish-Master and the Baby Cat (my favorite shape of L & S). All five of these were advertised in 1951 and the Baby Cat was advertised as new in 1951. The Panfish-Master certainly was in full production by 1951 also.

The earliest lures had opaque eyes in various colors such as red eyes with black irises, red/yellow, and white/black, and the eyes were part of the mold. My photos clearly show the differences in eyes and in hardware styles. Some people think that the new eye style came with the 1954 molding equipment but this is wrong, The new eyes were in use in all models by 1951 (1951 advertising documents this; they were advertised as "life-like fish eyes" in the literature). But, with the new molding equipment came new opaque lure finishes and new sizes. By 1950 the company had already started making lures at the Clearwater, Florida, location to cover the southern part of the country. At first they just added a new saltwater version but by 1952 they had developed a whole new line of "MirrOLures." The MirrOLure line added some sizes and the well-known reflective material under a translucent plastic exterior to give the lures the "built in flash" that made them famous. In 1970 Phil Schriner sold his portion of the company and it was reformed in Largo, Florida, where it is still in operation today.

I cannot emphasize too much how the lures of this company typify what has happened in lure collecting. I could walk through any lure show in 1995 and purchase L & S lures for $2.00 – 6.00 each without any trouble. I did a lure show the weekend of April 16, 2004, and the least expensive L & S lure I found was $8.00 in poor shape. The lures averaged $10.00 – 14.00 loose and $15.00 – 25.00 in boxes. Most of the ones in boxes had been re-boxed and were in the wrong ones, e.g. Panfish-Masters in Bass-Master boxes, etc. I have sold at least 50 online the past year averaging well over $8.00 each, and the better ones reached $40.00 (rare Gantron green Pike-Master). Clean pre-1951 models with opaque eyes new in the box with papers should start at $25.00 and will reach $50.00 if the collector needs the color or model.

Again, Baby Boomers fished with these lures. They are recent enough to be available but ones in mint condition or in boxes are not really that common. There is a wide variety of box types, eye types, lip types, model types, and colors. This is the formula for a popular lure collectible as color collecting is a major driving force for collectors.

I have always liked the lures — they are classic in design and colorful. My wife Wendy is an excellent barometer of collecting and she liked them in 1995 too, so I should have known they would go up in value! She was right about Cisco Kids, L & S, Doll Top Secrets, Hellbenders, and many more. But the reality is that all of these lures have the same formula stated above and this increases interest in a lure or a company.

The first photo shows a very early diving lip and details the opaque eye style on a Bass-Master lure. The large teddy bear type glass eyes were added in 1951 so we know this is 1946 – 1950 production. Somewhere in the 1950 – 1954 era the numbering also changed on the lures and eventually the lettering was on the front of the diving lip, not the rear. $25.00+ due to early year and excellent condition.

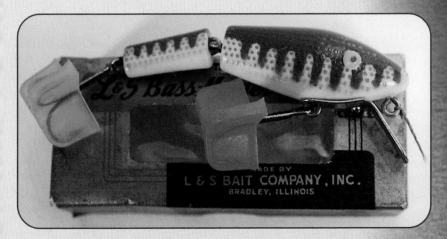

Another opaque eye early Bass-Master lure shown on its box. I left the line tie on to show that even fished this lure still is in nice shape, actually excellent to excellent minus condition. This is one of many box types. Even after adding the Clearwater, Florida, operation, not all boxes had the address added. This is also one of the first of the standard color designs. $30.00 – 40.00 boxed.

A comparison of a Pike-Master on the bottom, Bass-Master on the top, and Panfish-Master in the middle. All were in production with these eyes in 1951 so they could all be 53+ years old already. $12.00 – 15.00 loose.

One of my personal favorite L & S lures, the Baby Cat. This lure was introduced in 1951 it is an early one in an early box. This is Model 7C38, 3¼", ⁹⁄₁₆ oz. $25.00 – 35.00.

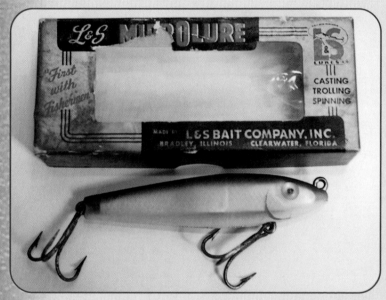

A little newer but still an earlier MirrOLure from the Florida location. Model 7M27 FLOATER is stamped on its belly. The lure needs a little cleaning but is in excellent condition. $20.00 – 25.00 boxed.

Luhr Jensen & Sons

Luhr Jensen & Sons, Hood River, Oregon, was detailed in my *Volume 1*, and it is famous for its early recognition of spinning tackle importance. Early spinning lures include the Wobl-Lure, Ford Fenders, Knobby Spoons, and many more. Its drift-floating bobber is still common. The Knobby-Wobbler lure is a single-hook spoon with hammering to protrude part of the spoon. Spinning lures included the Doo-Dad in ⅟₃₀ oz., ⅟₂₀ oz. and ⅟₁₀ oz. varieties from 1⅜" to 2⅛" long. The Doo-Dad also came in a ⅙ oz., 2⅞" size suitable for light casting. It could also be used with spinning tackle as could the lighter models of the Doo-Dad.

Luhr Jensen should likely be considered one of the "big seven" if we look at the company since 1980. Likely, it is now one of the "big two," Luhr Jensen and Pradco. As did Pradco, Jensen was quick to buy out small companies, companies in economic distress, companies with one good lure in its line of lures, and companies in direct competition. Between Luhr Jensen and Pradco, most of our traditional collectible lure companies are now owned by one of them.

But for the early years, prior to 1980, Luhr Jensen made far fewer lures that have become collectible. Some of them include: early salmon plugs, their first versions of the Eddie Pope Hot Shot lures, some of the early metal baits it was the first to make for spinning, and some of the first Oreno lures it made after owning the rights to the lures after buying the Glen L. Evans company of Idaho.

Regardless of one's collecting interests, there are likely some lures one will find that are Luhr Jensen or are now owned by the company that one wants to collect. Certain collectors 50 years from now will be interested in many of the lures this company has produced since 1980, as well as the ones from 1937 until 1980.

Luhr Jensen started by hammering out metal spoons and spinners allegedly from Ford Fenders and so named an early lure. These are fairly early examples of small metal baits new in bags (except lower right mixture). I sold quite a few of these older bags for a few dollars each. $2.00 – 5.00 per small bag.

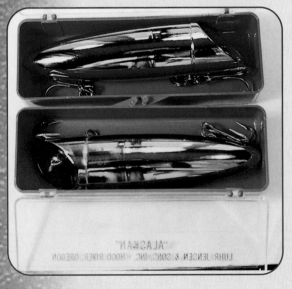

The Alaskan salmon lure was purchased by Luhr Jensen and it continued production for a while or repackaged them for sale. The Alaskan is actually in the middle range of rarity for salmon plugs so these are a nice find. I sold a few for $25.00 – 40.00 each new in the box. They were in three colors, gold, silver, and copper. $25.00 – 50.00 each.

Luhr Jensen also bought out the Eddie Pope Company and its successful Hot Shot lure. This is one of many styles of cards for the Hot Shot. $12.00 – 20.00, depending on color and age.

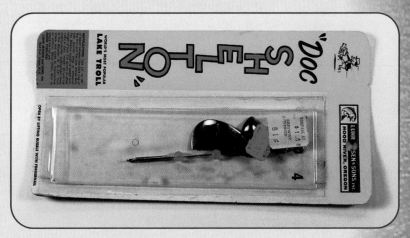

Even older carded lures such as the common Doc Shelton have sold well lately to collectors. $6.00 – 9.00.

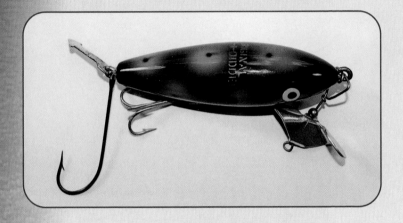

A prototype Nip-I-Diddee lure from Luhr Jensen? Older with "Original" still present, odd spinner, single hook, pork rind attachment, front hook holes plugged, 3" long. This lure came from Hood River region, home to Luhr Jensen. Luhr Jensen acquired the rights to the Oreno line of lures when buying out Glen L. Evans company in 1982. They currently make Bass-Orenos, Babe-Orenos, Nip-I-Diddees and Spin-I-Diddees, and others. The lure shown was never placed into production to my knowledge. A visit to the Internet site of www.luhrjensen.com will lead one to a complete history of the company and list all of the other companies purchased by it over the years. $50.00 – 100.00+ if prototypical.

Marathon Bait Company

The Marathon Bait Company, Wausau, Wisconsin, was featured in *Volume 2* of my series and made extensive spinning and terminal tackle. Its spoon line was very complete and often the spoons have the telltale double spinner blades as tails on them. Other companies copied Marathon but the double tail spinner is typical of them. Two spoons being marketed in 1952 included the Jako Spoon and the Dictator Spoon, both in a variety of sizes designed for baitcasting and trolling. Marathon also marketed a complete line of Bear Valley, Slim Eli, Indiana, Colorado, and Idaho type spinners. Early spinning lures included a plunker type made for spinning available only in red/white that shows up often and it also made many weighted casting baits including the famous Musky-Houn, the Musk-E-Munk, and the shallow running Fish-Houn.

Marathon was a large competitor of Weber and Worth, both included in this guide. It is virtually impossible to cover all of its hundreds of spinners, fly rod baits, and other baits in a book of this nature. However, most of its baits are fairly common but be aware that a few are highly desired by collectors and a variety is shown here.

Marathon is best known for its spinners, spoons, and metal baits, and this shows a wide variety of them. Most metal lures are not in great demand. $5.00 – 10.00 unless boxed or very early examples.

Likely the most collectible of the wooden lures by Marathon is the Musk-E-Munk in either glass, tack, or decal eyes. The ones shown here have decal eyes and the top one is 2¾" long and from the late 1950s, the others are 2½" long and from the early 1950s. These were preceded by tack eye models and even earlier glass-eyed models. $50.00 – 75.00; range for early models would be $75.00 – 150.00+.

Millsite Tackle Co.

Millsite Tackle Co., Howell, Michigan, was detailed in depth in *Volume 1* of my series of books and recent information from a family member has added even more history. In 1952 all of its plastic baits (the company never made a wooden bait since beginning in 1938) were in full production along with the Daisy Fly Box and some other items. A simple surface popper called the Bassor was available in two sizes, ½ oz. and ⅝ oz. and 2¼" and 2¾" lengths. One of the most collectible Millsite lures is the Paddle Plug (often referred to as a Paddle Bug by collectors). This surface only lure was ½ oz., 1¾" long with a single treble hook. It looked like a large plastic beetle. Floating/diving lures included the wide variety of Millsite Minnows in nearly the same variations as the Heddon River Runts and the Deep Creep, Millsites version of a deep diving runt type lure. In addition, the other very collectible Millsite bait is the Rattlebug, a ⅝ oz., 1⅞" lure with an internal rattle and a single treble hook, also in the form of a plastic beetle (it predates the Paddle Plug). Another floating/diving lure was the Daily Double, an inverted "v" shaped lure made of plastic that had its diving depth controlled by hooking onto one end versus the other on the lure itself. The Daily Double is not only collectible but it is also still a bass catching lure and I have sold many for fishing at $15.00 – 20.00 each.

Millsite made a lot of lures and they show up often. Many of them are not marked, but many of them are marked. The Dapper Dan by Shakespeare is nearly identical to the Millsite runt styles.

Millsite lures are assuredly in the top 25 of lure demand by collectors. New in the box Paddle Plugs with hang tags have sold for up to $100.00 online the past two years. Daily Doubles always bring $15.00 – 30.00+. The Rattle Bugs sell for $30.00 – 50.00 loose. The early runt styles bring $15.00 – 30.00 for most of the lures, much more boxed. The other lures also do well as do the related fishing accessories. The rare pocket log recently sold for over $100.00 online. Even the fish-stringer, Millsite's oldest and first product, brings a decent price.

Box end and lure with hang tag, new from box for a Model 817 Daily Double lure in Bass/Pike size, e.g. not Muskie. As stated previously, this lure is in demand by both collectors and anglers as it really does work! Loose lures sell for $15.00 – 20.00 in fine shape and boxed ones should bring $25.00 – 40.00, depending on color.

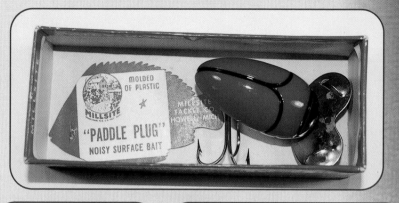

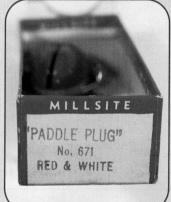

Views of a new in box Paddle Plug, No. 671, Red & White with insert, simple wire hook hangers, middle box end pattern. Sold online in 2002 for $85.00. Paddle plugs are in high demand and bring $40.00 – 60.00 loose, $50.00 – 100.00 boxed.

A photo to show the differences among the Rattle Bug on the left, Paddle Plug in the center, and even older Beetle Bug on the right. $40.00 – 60.00 loose, $50.00 – 100.00 boxed.

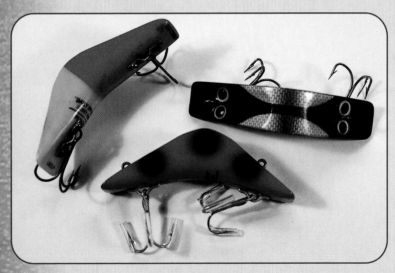

Three typical color patterns shown on Bass-Pike sized Daily Double lures. $15.00 – 20.00 loose, $25.00 – 40.00 boxed.

Top lure is a 3" long, painted eye, simple screw hardware. Dapper Dan by Shakespeare, bottom, is a Millsite. $15.00 – 25.00 loose per lure. Add $15.00 for boxes.

Two sizes of Millsite minnows in same color pattern, 3" and 2⅜" long. Unlike the Dapper Dan, these early Millsites had slight indentations in the eye sockets. Later Millsites had flush painted eyes. $20.00+ loose for these early ones in this color; double if boxed.

Millsite Beetle, 1" body, spinner says Bug Bait, Pat's All'd & Pend, Millsite Beetle, and Howell, Mich. One of the few metal baits collected in earnest. $35.00 – 60.00 loose, doubled if boxed.

181

Pachner and Koller (P&K)

Pachner and Koller produced plastic and rubber collectible baits. Offerings include the deep diving Amazin' Mazie at ⅝ oz., 3", Bright Eyes at ½ oz., 2¾", the surface plunker Walkie Talkie lure at ½ oz., 3", and a variety of rubber lures. Rubber lures include Softy the Crab in two sizes at ½ oz. and ⅝ oz., Spotty the Frog at ⅝ oz., and the Mouse lure, available in both casting at ⅝ oz. and fly rod sizes. They also made a Shiner lure in ⅝ oz. size.

These lures have become very popular with collectors the past five years. The Bright Eyes sold for $5.00 at lure shows in 1995 and now sells for $15.00 at least. The boxed plunker type Walkie Talkie sells for $30.00 – 50.00 if mint in box. The Amazin' Mazie does as well. The Whirlaway is in high demand by collectors selling easily for $25.00+ without a box. The rubber lures bring a little less. One will certainly find some of these lures and one should know they are of value to collectors. The shapes are unusual and the marketing was quite vigorous so the lures are fairly easy to find. But, they were fished heavily, so finding them in excellent to mint is an important consideration for a lure of this recent vintage (1940s – 1960s).

A beautiful green scale Amazin' Mazie lure in excellent shape. $25.00 – 35.00, more if boxed.

P&K Popper on card, catalog No. 3P, size #4. Rare find, $35.00+.

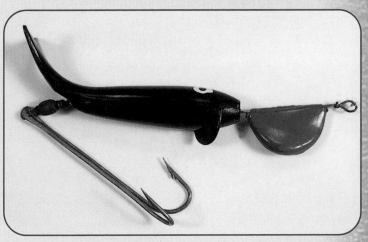

P&K Whirlaway, 2¾" long, painted eyes, 2" line tie wire is missing on this one. $15.00 – 20.00. $25.00+ if intact and $40.00+ if boxed.

P&K Walkie Talkie, new from two-piece box, Cat. No. 43-P. $15.00 – 20.00 loose; $30.00+ boxed.

P&K Walkie Talkie Junior. More uncommon than larger size. $15.00 – 20.00 loose, $30.00 boxed.

Phillips Fly & Tackle Co.

The Phillips Fly & Tackle Co., Alexandria, Pennsylvania, produced the Crippled Killer surface lure in plastic in a ½ oz., 2¾" size, a ¼ oz., 2¼" size, and a ⅜ oz., 1¾" size in 1952. In addition, this company was well established in the fly and spinning tackle trade already by 1952.

The Flash-O-Minnow was an attractive plastic minnow with foil inserts and came in a ¼ oz., 1¾" size. The Forty-Niner surface popper was ¼ oz. and 2" long. The Invincible Feather Minnow was an original fly rod offering increased to ⅛ oz. size for spinning. The Invincible Streamer Fly followed suit at ⅛ oz. The Midget Killer was a smaller sized Crippled Killer at ¼ oz. and only 1³⁄₁₆" long. Phillips also made the Spin Devil in ¼ oz., 2¼" length, the Spin Popper in ¼ oz., 2" length and the Spino-Mino in only ⅛ oz. and 1¼" length and ¼ oz. and 3½" length. Finally, they offered a Weedless Popper at ¼ oz. and 2½" length (double weed guard and hackle single hook). Phillips spinning baits were made in plastic and came in a variety of beautiful colors, many with foil inserts. Early Phillips products came in two-piece cardboard boxes and in the 1950s Phillips made a transition to a hinged plastic box for its lures. I recently found six dozen early 1950s Phillips spinning lures in an estate sale and they all sold for $25.00 or more each, new in the boxes, online in 2003.

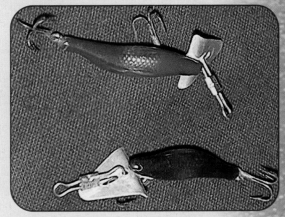

A photo of two unmarked Rainbow Runner lures. $15.00 – 25.00 for these colors.

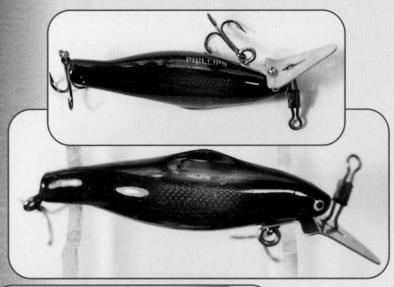

Phillips Spinning lure examples. $15.00 – 25.00 boxed, $8.00 – 15.00 loose. I sold over 25 of the boxed Phillips plastic lures in late 2003 and they averaged over $25.00 each. The gold foil one is called a Rainbow Runner.

186

Eddie Pope & Company

Eddie Pope & Company was located in Montrose, California, and is now owned by Luhr Jensen. This West Coast company invented the famed Hot Shot lure that is still being used to catch fish from trout to monster salmon. By 1952, Pope was marketing a ¼ oz. version of its Hot Shot lure as a spinning lure. At that time it would have come in a two-piece plastic box. Later in the 1950s it was carded on an attractive card showing a fishing scene. Some of these carded versions have sold online for $20.00 – 30.00 each for better colors.

The baitcasting size of the Hot Shot was ⅝ oz., 3¼" long and is still being made and sold by Luhr Jensen today. It was packaged in a two-piece plastic box. It was designed as a deep diving lure with an extended diving plane and it cast like a bullet. It was made of plastic as was its ¼ oz. counterpart used for spinning. The colors for the Pope Hot Shots are not identical to today's colors, and these lures are also collectible, valued at $15.00 – 20.00 or more, new in the box.

Pope lures do not show up as often as some shown in this book but are very common lures on the West Coast and even in some other regions. But one should be aware of the lures and the pretty blue cards on which they came for a while.

New in the box 3¼" Orange with papers, first box, Model M102. $20.00+ in new condition, as shown.

New on card 521 D Gold Plate small Hot Shot lure, pre-zip code card. This is the one that is trading very well, with sales hitting nearly $30.00 each. $20.00 – 30.00 carded.

Three older fly rod models, two 2⅛" M5 Models and an M3. $4.00 – 6.00 each, loose.

Fishback Model 4 Sinker in Purple Scale, 2½" long. These are again being made by Luhr Jensen but the early Pope ones sell for $12.00 – 16.00 loose.

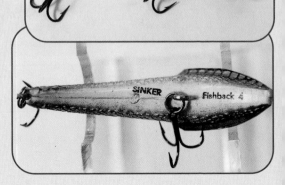

R-Jay Industries (Brook's Baits)

R-Jay Industries from Ohio made a number of nice early plastic baits that are just now gaining the recognition they deserve as more and more collectors discover them. The Brook's No. 4 and No. 7 weighted casting baits, similar to some by Foss and others, are very attractive. The No. 7 was a ½ oz., 4" lure with a large 3/0 weedless single hook and the No. 4 weighed ⅝ oz. at 4" with a 4/0 weedless single hook. The Brook's Double O came in both a straight version at ½ oz., 2½" and a Jointed version at ½ oz. and 3 ½" length. The Double O was a plastic fish-shaped lure with a diving bill and protruding eyes, and some also came with a scale pattern embedded in the plastic. They also made a popper called the Brook's No. 5 at ½ oz., 2½" length. It had a very large open mouth, protruding eyes, and two trebles, and was made of plastic as were all of R-Jay Industries' baits. The popper was available in a spinning size at some point.

Likely the most common bait found in the field from this company is the Brook's Reefer, a jointed plastic banana-shaped lure. These are common in the Midwest and likely nationally as they were distributed and advertised nationally. Many of these are in beautiful colors and they came in both spinning and casting weights and sizes.

Most of the Brook's baits trade for $8.00 – 20.00 at this time, so one can still afford to seek them out. I think the company will continue to gain in popularity with collectors.

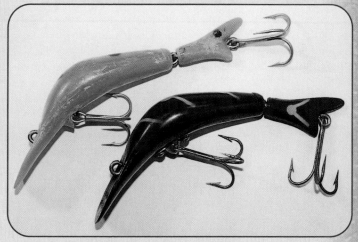

Brooks Reefers in two colors. Note the mildew on the orange one; it comes right off with water. Both lures are actually in excellent shape. $8.00 – 20.00 depending on color/condition. These are both common colors with the black being a little less common.

Rinehart Tackle Co.

It is generally believed that the Rinehart Tackle Co. was started in 1940 or 1941 in Newark, Ohio. Over the years the company moved its operation at least twice, once to Gahanna and then to Marietta, both in Ohio. Its Jinx lures are a challenge to collect because of color variations far beyond their standard catalog color listings. Except for solid and bi-color lures there are slight color differences in Rinehart lures, almost to the point where no two are alike. Even with the published catalog colors, there were over 80 color patterns, considering that they were offered in transparent, not transparent, and luminous. Its most common lure was the Jinx, in both bass and Musky sizes. A saltwater version of the Musky size was called the Surfcaster and the lure is scarce, as is the Spinner version, the Buzzer.

The rarest of this company's productions, however, was the Chief and the Chubby. One might describe the Chubby as a pregnant Jinx, or river runt type. The Chief was a river runt type and it is believed that it was made in five sizes.

The molded plastic bodies were contracted from a Frazerburg, Ohio, company and over the years we have found several body variations, including: the length and width of the lures, eye and hook locations, type of hook hangers, and the angle of noses and body slant. In the early years, they also made rubber and deer hair Natural Life Flyrod lures.

I covered this company in *Volume 2* and added many more details not included here in my *Volume 3*. I include this company in this guide as the lures are common and collector interest has really grown the past five years. The lures trade commonly for $15.00 – 30.00 loose and more if boxed. The Musky size lures are valued even more and the earliest blue/white boxes add even more value to the package. Lures such as the Chubby would trade for $100.00 or more as they are very rare. But, one will likely find a Jinx or two when first starting to collect, and it's important to be aware of their value and designs.

The Rinehart Chubby. $100.00+.

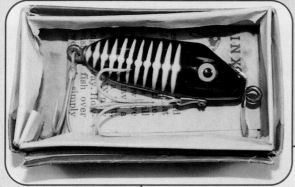

Newer, but still pre-zip, likely the 1950s, version of the Rinehart box, green and yellow, with a black with white rib shore pattern Jinx, Model 10M 475, made of Tenite, price of $1.09, raised molded eyes, opposite box end stamped WRB; and the lure's hook hardware. $30.00 in box minimum, $15.00 loose.

191

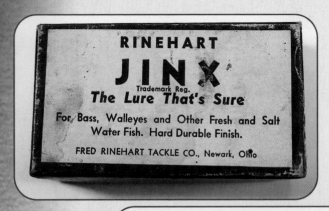

An older Jinx box in white and blue and its contents, a Luminous white with black ribs Jinx Lure, 2¼" long, rare color. This older box with a rare luminous color would bring over $50.00 in this condition.

A tough to find Musky size, 4¹³⁄₁₆" long, Jinx in a simple rainbow pattern, surface belly, screw/washer tail hardware, and raised molded eyes. I paid $40.00 for it in early 2001 in a private sale.

C. C. Roberts

The C. C. Roberts Company, Mosinee, Wisconsin, is famous for its Muskie lure known as the Mud Puppy. However, it also made a great bass-sized casting lure known as the Pupette that came in a beautiful black and yellow two-piece cardboard box. The Mud Puppy came in two sizes and two models. The sizes were 2 oz., 7" for the Mud Puppy and 1¼ oz., 5" for the Little Mud Puppy. They came in "lake" and "river" models. The lake model had a detachable hook that actually allowed the fish to shake the lure loose and after landing the trophy Muskie the lure would be retrieved from the water. The river model had permanent hooks so the lure would remain with the fish. The Pupette was a surface wobbler with a diving lip to make it wobble-shaped, similar to a Bass-Oreno type lure. It was ¾ oz., 2⅞" long, with two trebles. Roberts also made an experimental fly rod Mud Puppy never put into production (shown in our *Captain John's Fishing Tackle Price Guide*), and duck and goose decoys for family members and friends documented in my book on the same subject and in *Volume 2* of my series. The Mud Puppy lures are very collectible but the Pupette is far harder to find and would be a nice addition to any collection. The lures were all made of wood.

Mud Puppy lures often trade for $50.00 – 75.00, and early ones with glass eyes will bring up to $200.00. Boxed lures with the nice cartoon boxes often sell for over $100.00 as well. Boxed Pupette lures trade for $35.00 – 60.00 and they are hard to find. Technically, I could not decide if I should include this company as one will not find as many of these lures as others in this book. However, I think of most of the Muskie lure manufacturers, this is the most obvious choice to include in a field guide.

"Cartoon Box" with new-in-box Perch pattern Mud Puppy, river version, Model 0102-L.M.P.-R.M. $40.00+.

Comparison of a River version Perch with a Lake version Natural, Model 0100-L.M.P., Mud Puppies. These are actually "Little Mud Puppies" at 5½", 1¼ oz., and the Mud Puppies were 7" at 2 oz. The River version has permanent hooks; the Lake version has a hook that allows the Muskie to throw the bait itself, and the hook harness would then come free of the lure and stay with the fish. This prevented hooked fish, in theory anyway, from escaping. Once the fish was landed, the fisherman would find the lure, reassemble, and be back in business. $40.00+ each, new in boxes.

194

Wallsten Tackle

The Cisco Kid line of lures has become one of my favorites, and my wife Wendy's too, and is rapidly becoming a hot category for collectors. If one handles the lures it becomes readily apparent why: they are quality through and through! The paint on them is exceptional and the designs are flawless; there is simply something about the shape and design elements that not only was attractive to fish (they really worked), but also to collectors. Some of the prices paid for rare and early Cisco Kid lures are comparable with rare Heddons. The beautiful two-piece cardboard box is very rare and the dealer carton is even more difficult to find. The original Topper is rare. Many of the early lures are difficult to find. Some of the lures being sold in the early 1950s include: Injured Cisco, ½ oz., 3½"; Midget Cisco Kid, ⅜ oz., 2¼", Musky Cisco Kid, 1¼ oz., 6¼" and the Cisco Kid at ⅝ oz., 3½" long. I just documented this company in *Volume 3* of my Modern Lure series and one should see it for extensive details. Other lures of note are the Cisco Topper, the Cisco Topper, Jr., the Skip-N-Cisco, the Model 1100 saltwater bait, the Husky Cisco Kid (Musky Cisco with changes), and many more.

Values on these lures five years ago were in the same range as many plastic lures, $5.00 – 10.00. However, they have come of age and some recent examples of sales top three figures, with one Topper selling online for $256.00 in March of 2004. Most Toppers still trade for $25.00 – 50.00, but early ones without the spinner and/or Flaptail bring good money. Rare colors also may bring $60.00 – 80.00 on any of the lures. Some lures are still very common, such as the Model 1100, and will not sell for much over $20.00 regardless of color. Musky Cisco Kids sell for $25.00 – 100.00+, depending on age, box, color, and more.

As a company, Wallsten no longer exists. However, the lures are still being made by Suick of Wisconsin. Suick owns the rights to the line now. Many of the colors are the same, so be careful, make sure you know what you are buying!

Rare style Cisco Kid Topper without spinner or flap tail. It is 3⅞" long, has surface belly hardware, screw tail hardware, and painted eyes, and is marked on the back. I sold it and the next item for $1,000.00 in 2003.

Very rare dealer carton with one new in box Model 7 C-Orange 2½" long lure with no name on diving lip yet. This sold for $1,000.00 by private sale along with the rare Topper on page 195 in 2003.

A Model 500, Jointed Cisco Kid in orange coach dog; 2½" long, ⅜ oz. lure above the Musky Cisco Kid (marked on belly); and the later Husky Cisco Kid (not marked and no inverted bell tail cap). $40.00+ for Jointed Cisco Kid, $25.00+ for Musky, $15.00 for Husky.

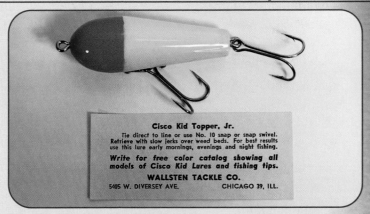

Cisco Kid Topper, Jr.
Tie direct to line or use No. 10 snap or snap swivel.
Retrieve with slow jerks over weed beds. For best results
use this lure early mornings, evenings and night fishing.
*Write for free color catalog showing all
models of Cisco Kid Lures and fishing tips.*
WALLSTEN TACKLE CO.
5405 W. DIVERSEY AVE.   CHICAGO 39, ILL.

A transitional Cisco Kid Topper, Jr., as it was evolving in 1954 from the Topper, Jr. to the Injured Cisco. $40.00.

Model 700, Cisco Kid Topper lure, a more common example than on the previous page, but not as common as the ones with a flap tail and front spinner only. $50.00 – 100.00.

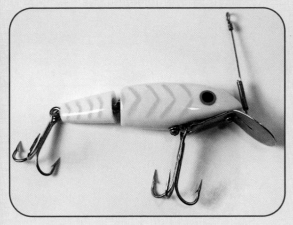

A beautiful and rare color Model 500, Jointed Cisco Kid in Yellow Shore (Model 500YS). $90.00 – 110.00.

197

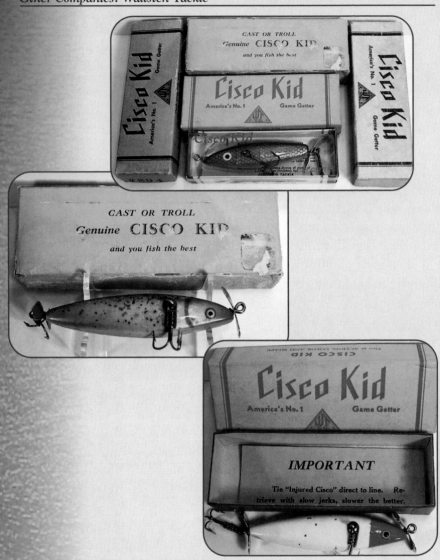

A photo essay showing the history of the Injured Cisco Kid and its box types. The yellow box is the first box and it is very, very rare, pre-1948, valued at $300.00 with the lure shown. The orange box and the associated lure is pre-1949; notice the crimped hooks. It is valued at $225.00. The blue/white box is from 1949 to 1952 – 1953 and it and the lure are valued at $120.00. The last two-piece box is the turquoise box from 1953 – 1954, and it is valued at $120.00 also. The modern box is the common green/yellow box with plastic top, which was used from 1954 – 1964; however, Model 819 is a rare color green/gold Injured Cisco, making the set worth $80.00. This is a 1964 lure in a Chicago box with a Florida insert.

Weber Lifelike Fly Co.

Weber Lifelike Fly Co., Stevens Point, Wisconsin, was the largest producer of fly rod fishing tackle in America at one time. Started by Carrie Frost in the late 1800s and in business officially until 1988, this company was detailed in *Modern Fishing Lure Collectibles, Volume 1*. Of all fly companies, it is the most obvious to be included in this guide as the lures are common but often not identified.

Some of its early spinning entries included the Mitey-Mite Devon, nearly identical to an Airex Brown-Terrible lure, the Weberkraft spinner with a streamer attached, and the Tailspin lure with a little spinner blade following a weighted streamer. Weber was one of the largest, if not the largest, producers of terminal tackle, spinners, spoons, and spinning lures in the 1950s. Its Mr. Champ Spoon is famous and was knocked-off by many other companies due to its success. In 1952 it was available in ¼ oz., ½ oz., and ⅞ oz. sizes for spinning, casting, and trolling. The Tiger King was a weighted casting bait made by Weber designed for shallow running, similar to a Jamison Tiger Cat. Weber also made two underwater weighted casting baits called the Outlaw and the Rowdy.

Weber did not produce many baitcasting lures but did have a few, with the Dive-N-Wobl being a great example and highly desired by collectors ($100.00+). Also, Weber made many plastic baits similar to lures made by other companies and lures of its unique design. Many of the plastic spinning baits are in demand, such as the Shadrac, the Dylite Spinning Mouse, and the Spin Frog or the Flip Frog lures.

Weber also made extensive fly rod items, flies, lures, spinners, reels, rods, and nearly all types of terminal tackle. The company also made the rare Cat hand catapult developed by another company and purchased by Weber for marketing.

Other common lures to find include the neat little Mystic spinning lure similar to a Pico, Bayou Boogie, or even more on point, a South Bend Optic. Also look for the Bottom Knocker, Little Sam, Swim King, Bass Bomb, and Big-Burp Popper.

Weber also sold a Fifi lure similar to the imported Vivif lure, and had an endless supply of spoons similar to Dardevle lures and many others. Its own spoon, the Champ, was copied by at least two other companies due to its success. Weber sold beetles similar to Millsite beetles and so many flies it would take a hundred pages or more to list them all.

I am fortunate in owning many of the original archival pieces of the company, including most of the 217 archival cards kept in files to examine by workers when tying flies or making lures. Many of the cards are one-of-a-kind and have the writing of the Weber manager on them,

199

instructing workers how to prepare a lure or fly. I have sold these cards for $50.00 – 300.00 each for the most part. I also have many lures being developed at the time of the company closing.

Weber is one of my choices to be in the "top of the top" of companies due to its size, its distribution channels, its great lure making history going back to the 1800s, and its impact on both using fly rod baits for casting and spinning. Add to this the fact that Weber recognized the role of spinning as rapidly or moreso than most companies and responded with many collectible products. Seldom will one find old tackle without a Weber item or two being present. See my *Volume 1* for a complete and detailed history showing hundreds of examples and rare archival material.

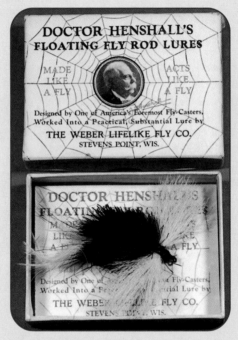

An early Weber box and fly with the nice spiderweb design. $75.00 – 125.00.

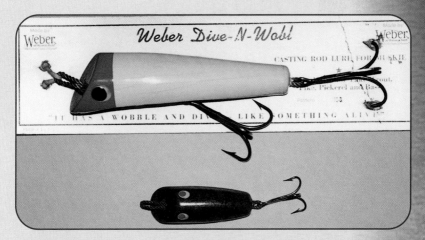

The rare Weber Dive-N-Wobl lures, large one new on card. This card was inserted into a two-piece cardboard box. $100.00+; $150.00+ with box.

A bevy of collectible Weber spinning and fly rod baits. Top row shows the Dylite Big-Burp Popper, Spin-Frog, an unusual color in a Weedless Mousie, and two Dylite Mice. The bottom row shows the four-leg frog, the crawdad, a Little Sam, and three Pop-N-Wigl lures. Each of these is worth $15.00 – 20.00, and the yellow Spin-Frog and rare color mouse will bring more.

Wood Mfg. Co.

The Wood Mfg. Co., El Dorado, Arkansas, manufactured a number of collectible baits. I recently expanded my coverage of this lure company in my *Volume 3* on modern lures as it is becoming so popular with collectors. Also, the lures were in wide distribution and will be found in many locations. It offered many collectible plastic baits and advertised widely beginning in 1947.

By 1952, Wood offered the Deep-R-Doodle in ⅕ oz. size (Model 300) and the Dipsy Doodle in ¼ oz., 2½" length (Model 1400). Likely the most desired of Wood's lures is the Spot Tail Minnow. It was available in ⅜ oz. with two trebles (Model 700), ½ oz. (Model 1100), and a jointed Spot Tail at ½ oz. (Model 1300). The Model 800 Deep-R-Doodle was ½ oz. and the Model 1000 Deep-R-Doodle was ⅝ oz. and 3" long. The Model 1500 Dipsy Doodle was ⅜ oz. and 3" long. The surface Model 1600 Doodler was a ½ oz. bait.

Some of the lures such as the metal Arkansas Wiggler are very hard to find and have recently sold for $80.00+ online. Lures new in the 1947 two-piece cardboard boxes with pocket catalogs often trade for $60.00 – 80.00. I recently (early 2004) sold a Spot Tail Minnow in only very good minus condition for nearly $20.00 online. Mint and excellent ones will bring $25.00 – 35.00 without boxes. Again, as with many companies since the war, many Baby Boomers are interested in these lures since they fished with them.

A 1947 box, pocket catalog insert, and a Dipsy Doodle in Smokey Joe color, new in box. Online sales have been as high as $80.00 for a similar set. Range of $50.00 – 80.00 expected.

A closer view of the larger Dipsy Doodle next to the smaller but heavy Model 300 Deeper Doodle. Both lures are excellent and the green scale is a rarer color. $20.00 – 30.00 each, without boxes.

A look at the Spot Tail minnow as shown on a 1947 box. Box alone, $10.00 – 15.00; with lure, $50.00+.

The Worth Company

The Worth Company, Stevens Point, Wisconsin, was featured in my *Volume 2* with many catalog pages reprinted and lures shown. This company made hundreds of spinners, spoons, spinning baits, and an extensive terminal tackle line. Worth made a number of Trolling Spoons with a single shaft, beads, dressed treble hooks, and a Colorado type spinner blade. Worth was also a major supplier of June Bug spinners and June Bug trolling spoons with dressed trebles. Two of the more famed spoons include the Water Demon, two of which were spinning sizes, and the Fishdevl in both casting and spinning sizes. Also, similar to Weber, Worth offered a complete line of weighted streamer flies designed for spinning.

The company did not offer too much in baitcasting but as one of the "big three" providers of spinners they need to be mentioned. The "big three" are Marathon, Weber, and Worth, all Wisconsin bait companies. Some would argue we should include H-I and Pflueger, but I consider them simply large lure companies, not just primarily spinner and fly producers.

One of the most desired Worth lures is the Flutter Fin as shown here. $20.00 – 35.00 loose; more if boxed.

Two boxed Flutter Fins, two box types. $40.00 – 60.00.

One of the most recognizable of the Worth spoons, the Water Demon and its box. $10.00 for spoon. Box and spoon, $25.00+.

Wright & McGill Co.

The Wright & McGill Co., located at 1463 York St., Denver, Colorado, in 1952 was the famed maker of Eagle Claw hooks and rods. The company also made a number of spinning baits, spinners, and spoons. The Bug-A-Boo was a plastic lure made in ⅛ oz., 1¾" size for spinning and a larger baitcasting size. The Miracle Minnow was available in ¼ oz., 1¾" size and also in ⅛ oz. 1¾" size by 1952. The Miracle Minnow was also available in a ⅜ oz., 1¾" length and a ⅜ oz., 2½" jointed model. The Hi-Jacker was another attractive lure made by this company worth collecting. The plastic baits sell for $8.00 – 16.00 loose commonly and sometimes more. I sold boxed baits online for upwards of $40.00 with the nice trout model of a jointed Miracle Minnow shown here selling for $48.00 new in the box.

Wright & McGill made a number of vintage baitcasting lures as well. Earlier models included the Bass-Nabber, Bass-O-Gram, Crawfish, Flapper Crab, Horsefly, Baby Mouse, Nicky Mouse, and the Shiner. Wright & McGill baitcasting lures are scarce compared to its plastic lures and to most lures put in this book, and sell in the $100.00 – 200.00 range.

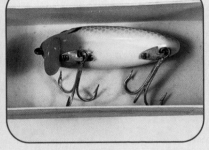

Miracle Minnows in their display type boxes. The Trout sold for nearly $50.00 on eBay in early 2002. The other lure should bring $30.00 – 50.00.

A second box type and its contents, surface hardware Bug-A-Boo. $20.00 – 30.00 boxed; $18.00 loose.

A nice color of Wright & McGill lure, 3" long, surface hardware, eyes carved into molding. $15.00 – 18.00 loose.

Summary

I must end somewhere and this is it for now. This was an easy book to write given the extensive data I have on lures, but nearly impossible to decide which companies to exclude. Many other companies should be in the book but space does not allow it. But, keep in mind my goal: *To show readers the most likely lures to be found in the field.*

It is my contention that about 80 – 90% of all lures found in the field today come from post-1940. Further, I believe that about 70% of all lures found in the field are from one of the big six companies featured in the beginning of this book. Then, I think the other companies in the second part of the book will cover at least 80% of the remaining 30%. In other words, I believe that this book will cover about 94% of all lures found in the field by volume. This is not determined scientifically but is based upon ten solid years of selling thousands upon thousands of collectible fishing lures.

I used 1952 as a benchmark and added earlier years and later years as well. I tried to break it up into spinning and baitcasting when possible. I have detailed the importance of vintage wooden lures being replaced by classic plastic lures. By the late 1940s, baitcasting was quickly giving way to spinning and spincasting was beginning to develop in earnest in the early 1950s. These developments have a direct impact on what was being made in the 1950s and now what we collect from the 1940s – 1960s.

I have not covered many fine companies. For instance Makinen Tackle was almost included but they did not advertise or distribute as heavily as some companies included. A most difficult decision was to leave out so many fine companies of recent vintage or small size.

Smaller companies to watch for include Bear Creek (also ice decoys), Buckeye Baits, Burke, Clark, Pico (Padre Island Company), Ropher of Fin-Dingo fame, Tackle Industries, Thompson of Doll Top Secret fame, and hundreds more.

Newer companies that are hot to collectors include many I have featured in detail in *Volume 3* such as Bagley's, Cotton Cordell lures, Poe's Super Cedar lures, Rebel lures of Pradco, Storm Lures, Smithwick Lures, and others.

Older, but less far reaching companies, such as Bingo Baits, Hump Lures, and Tulsa Tackle were recently detailed in separate sections in my *Volume 3*, but do not reach the national distribution level that I used as a selection point for companies in this book. However, collectors should soon find out about Bingo and Hump lures as they sell for

$20.00 – 60.00 each at this time. Also, both are excellent examples of Modern Era companies beginning in the late 1930s and evolving with only plastic lures.

And only because there is less general interest in metal lures did I exclude the companies of Eppinger, Hildebrandt, Hofschneider, Johnson, Kush, Skinner, and other large producers of metal lures. Eppinger also made a few wooden lures but they are not common outside of Michigan. Regardless, I chose to concentrate on the more collectible lures in this book so they were excluded. But, some of the early lures and boxes from any of these companies are now collectible. In early 2004 I sold an early Eppinger Osprey two-piece cardboard box for $26.00 online as one example.

I had to select a certain number of companies or we would have created another publishing nightmare in terms of length. Frankly, I do not think that collectors understand the costs to produce a volume such as this in 100% color and I am amazed that my publisher is so generous in the pricing. I thank Schroeder Publishing and Collector Books for bringing this to everyone and allowing me the chance to put it together.

I hope you have enjoyed the trip. I am always looking for new items to describe to future readers and I am also willing to buy collections or appraise items for collectors. I also always appreciate any paper items and contacts from company officials or family members of lure makers.

If you have items you want me to examine or if I may be of assistance in selling your collection, contact me via e-mail at findingo@netonecom.net or lewisr@ferris.edu. My user identification on eBay is findingo and you can always find me through it also.

Or, for those preferring to write or call, you may reach me at Dr. Russell E. Lewis, 515 Bishop Hall, Ferris State University, Big Rapids, MI 49307. You may leave a detailed message at my voicemail at 231-591-3581. I respond to all legitimate inquiries as rapidly as time allows. Good luck finding lures!

Other books by Russell E. Lewis:

Modern Fishing Lure Collectibles, Vol. 1, $24.95
Modern Fishing Lure Collectibles, Vol. 2, $24.95
Modern Fishing Lure Collectibles, Vol. 3, $24.95
Captain John's Fishing Tackle Price Guide, John A. Kolbeck and
    Russell E. Lewis, $19.95